# The SOUPMAKER'S KITCHEN

## How to Save Your Scraps, Prepare a Stock, and Craft the Perfect Pot of Soup

**ALIZA GREEN**

with Photography by Steve Legato

First published in the United States of America in 2013 by
Quarry Books, a member of
Quayside Publishing Group
100 Cummings Center
Suite 406-L
Beverly, Massachusetts 01915-6101
Telephone: (978) 282-9590
Fax: (978) 283-2742
www.quarrybooks.com
www.quarrySPOON.com

10 9 8 7 6 5 4 3 2 1

ISBN: 978-1-59253-844-7

Digital edition published in 2013
eISBN: 978-1-61058-775-4

**Library of Congress Cataloging-in-Publication Data available**


Design: Sporto
Photography: Steve Legato, stevelegato.com

Printed in China

# CONTENTS

Introduction . . . . . . . . . . . . . . . . . . . . . . . . . . . . . . . . . . . . . . . . . . . . . . . . . . . 4

Chapter 1:
## STOCKS: THE FOUNDATION . . . . . . . . . . . . . . . . . . . . . . . . . . . 6

Chapter 2
## CLEAR BROTH-BASED SOUPS . . . . . . . . . . . . . . . . . . . . . . 8

Chapter 3
## FISH AND SEAFOOD SOUP/STEWS . . . . . . . . . . . . . . . . . . 42

Chapter 4
## POTAGES, PURÉES, AND CREAMY BISQUES . . . . . . . . . . . . . . . 56

Chapter 5
## PANADES . . . . . . . . . . . . . . . . . . . . . . . . . . . . . . . . . . . . . . . . . . . . . 72

Chapter 6
## BEAN SOUPS . . . . . . . . . . . . . . . . . . . . . . . . . . . . . . . . . . . . . . . . 86

Chapter 7
## HEARTY SOUPS . . . . . . . . . . . . . . . . . . . . . . . . . . . . . . . . . . . . 104

Chapter 8
## CHOWDERS . . . . . . . . . . . . . . . . . . . . . . . . . . . . . . . . . . . . . . . . 122

Chapter 9
## CHILLED SOUPS . . . . . . . . . . . . . . . . . . . . . . . . . . . . . . . . . . . 132

Appendix of Additional Techniques . . . . . . . . . . . . . . . . . . . . . . . . . . . . . . . . . 144

Resources . . . . . . . . . . . . . . . . . . . . . . . . . . . . . . . . . . . . . . . . . . . . . . . . . . . 154

Acknowledgments . . . . . . . . . . . . . . . . . . . . . . . . . . . . . . . . . . . . . . . . . . . . . 155

About the Author . . . . . . . . . . . . . . . . . . . . . . . . . . . . . . . . . . . . . . . . . . . . . 156

About the Photographer . . . . . . . . . . . . . . . . . . . . . . . . . . . . . . . . . . . . . . . 156

Index . . . . . . . . . . . . . . . . . . . . . . . . . . . . . . . . . . . . . . . . . . . . . . . . . . . . . 157

# INTRODUCTION

SOUP, BEAUTIFUL SOUP, is the most basic of cooked foods, the universal cure-all, the best way to use small amounts of food that might otherwise be discarded, and is a dish that can always be stretched to feed one more.

Soupmaking is associated with ancient women's cooking. Men primarily did the fire cooking—grilling and roasting—and women did the water cooking—simmering soups and stews. Here, you'll follow the circle of soup, savoring suppers that can be sipped while saving money, minimizing waste, and living greener by working with the natural cycle of food from the market and the garden to the kitchen.

The word *soup*, once also spelled *soop*, evolved from *sop*, a word of German origin, meaning a chunk of bread soaked in liquid and eaten without utensils. Soup is closely related to the word *sup*, so supper was originally a simple meal that could be sipped at the end of the day. French Onion Soup (page 76), which originated in its current form in Paris in the eighteenth century, and Zuppa Pavese (page 74) are modern-day sops or panades.

We can make good soup from almost any group of ingredients if we pay attention to the balance of flavor and contrast of texture and color. The legend of stone soup holds a lesson that from next to nothing, something good can always be made. From liquid—water or broth—hot stones, a few humble vegetables such as cabbage or kale, an onion, a handful of grain, a few bits of leftover meat or bones, and seasonings such as fresh herbs or spices, we created an appetizing and nourishing soup. Many people have lost the art of soupmaking, relying on a can, box, or frozen package instead. Packaged soups are high in sodium and may contain preservatives and artificial flavorings—all avoided by making your own.

In Biblical times, legumes (such as chickpeas, fava beans, and lentils) along with grains (such as barley and wheat) formed the basis of simple, rib-sticking gruels and porridges not very different from the Greek Lentil Soup (page 96) and the Turkish Red Lentil Soup (page 98). Early soups in Europe and the New World were prepared in a cleaned animal hide filled with liquid and heated with hot stones. Later came cauldrons of clay, metal, or wood filled with a hodge podge of ingredients to make a substantial one-pot soup or stew to be sipped or sopped up with bread.

In early medieval kitchens, the cauldron or *pot-au-feu* (pot on the fire) was never emptied—instead, soup was ladled out and more food bits were added to make an "everlasting soup" in a pot that was only cleaned out in preparation for a fast day. In Europe during Renaissance times, most people lived on soup and bread; only the wealthy ate roasted meats. Northern European cultures developed fruit soups made with fresh or dried fruits, such as Chilled Apricot Soup with Star Anise (page 134).

In Arab-influenced Spain, cold salad–soups known as *gazpacho* developed in which cucumbers, green grapes or tomatoes, onion or garlic, olive oil, and vinegar would be chopped small or mashed up with bread or nuts acting as a thickener and olive oil and vinegar for seasoning. (See Golden Tomato Gazpacho with Smoked Paprika, page 138.)

Today's convenient bouillon cubes and powdered soups may be traced back to fourteenth century Magyar warriors. They boiled dried, salted beef until it was tender, and chopped and dried it into powder. Only hot water was needed to make a meal of this portable soup. By the nineteenth century, travelers such as Lewis and Clark carried highly-reduced "pocket soup" while exploring the American West.

Though soup may be fixed using all manner of convenience products, serving a simmering pot of soup made from scratch brings people of all ages together, creating aroma and anticipation. It can act as an elegant starter or form the basis for a hearty one-dish meal with some crusty bread. Half the fun of soupmaking is in the prep—the satisfaction of taking simple ingredients, perhaps root vegetables from the farmers' market or soaked dried legumes, and transforming them into a steaming pot of fragrant soup. Many soups, especially those made from beans, have better texture the second time around.

We use leftovers and trimmings to make stocks, which become the foundation of the next soup, which provides trimmings for the next stock. But not all soups call for stock. The frugal Tuscan cook makes Acquacotta Maremmana (page 83) starting with water. The vegan South Indian Tomato-Tamarind Rasam (page 36) is based on the cooking liquid with the broth from split yellow lentils.

Broaden your repertoire in the world of soups and you'll eat well while making the most of fresh ingredients without waste. Cook up a big pot of soup once a week to have hearty, healthy, delicious homemade fare that's ready in minutes. The recipes in this book make about 1 gallon (4 L) of soup, plenty for today with leftovers for tomorrow or to pack in containers for the freezer. And, what could be better than knowing you have a stock of homemade soup ready to serve after a long day at work?

## Tools for the Soupmaker

Investing in basic high-quality tools and pots will make soupmaking easier and more fun for a lifetime of cooking.

| | |
|---|---|
| Blender and/or Immersion blender | The better the blender, the smoother your soup. |
| Chef's knife | A knife with an 8-inch (20 cm) blade is easier to control. |
| Chinois and/or China cap and/or Sieve | To strain the stock |
| Kitchen string | A roll of heavy-duty cotton kitchen string is used to tie together a bouquet garni, or sprigs of herbs, for easy removal or to tie large chunks of meat for even cooking. |
| Fish pliers or needle-nose pliers | Indispensable for pulling out the pesky pin bones from fish |

| | |
|---|---|
| Food processor with grater/shredder plates | To shred vegetables and to make puréed soups |
| Heavy-bottomed soup pot (stainless steel or enameled cast iron) | For even cooking and less tendency to burn |
| Ice wand freezer gel packs, or ice cube trays | To chill stocks and soups quickly |
| Juicer, such as a Champion | Use for fruit soup and other cold soups. |
| Ladles | A 6-ounce (170 g) ladle is a useful size. |
| Large stock pot holding at least 2 gallons (8 L) | For making stock in large quantities |
| Mandoline and/or Japanese Benriner cutter | For neat, even slices and julienne—matchstick-cut—vegetables |
| Masking tape, labels, and markers | When freezing, always label what's inside. |
| Microplane zester | Best for grating citrus zests without any bitter white pith |
| Paring knife | For paring root vegetables and other tasks |
| Peeler | Get the best one you can find—you'll be using this tool frequently. |
| Pyrex measuring cups | Pint (475 ml) and quart (1 L)—useful for pouring and for quick measuring |
| Storage containers | Pint (475 ml), quart; (1 L), and 2-quart; (2 L) sizes are most useful |
| Ziplock freezer bags | Be sure to seal the top carefully. |
| Wire spider | For scooping foods cooking in water or oil |

# Chapter 1

# STOCKS: THE FOUNDATION

Every last bit of vegetable and protein contains nutrition and flavor waiting to be savored.

IN MOST GOOD KITCHENS, one of the chef's tasks is inspecting the trash cans to make sure that nothing useful is tossed out, whether the cores of sweet bell pepper, the skin of onions, the head of a fish, or the wing tips of chicken. We can learn from the masters and get every last bit of flavor by making our own stock, one of the most satisfying tasks in the kitchen.

## Save That Vegetable Cooking Water

Many of the nutrients and much of the flavor of vegetables is contained in their cooking water, so don't throw it out. Potatoes, corn, sweet potatoes, spinach, green beans, beets, mushrooms, squash, zucchini, cauliflower, leeks, and sweet bell peppers all taste good and will give you instant vegetable stock. The water from cooking cabbage, rutabagas, or turnips will be too strong to use for delicate soups. Save small amounts of liquid in a ziplock bag or a small freezer container until you have enough to be useful, making sure to date and label the package. This is best done with organic vegetables, as conventional vegetables may leach pesticides into the cooking water.

## The Roasting Juices Are the Best Part

If you're a meat eater, you will often have trimmings from either raw or cooked product. Turn them into homemade stock that is full of flavor with rich body. Put that roasted chicken carcass, or the bones from a roasted meat, and any juices that have dripped off into a pot, add cold water, and simmer until the remaining meat falls off the bone. After a few hours, add aromatic vegetable and tender herb trimmings and continue simmering.

## Stockmaker's Tips

- Start stock using cold water, which helps extract gelatinous collagen from meats that may be sealed in by hot water.
- Bring the stock up to a boil slowly, skimming away the fat and impurities that rise to the surface.
- Simmer the stock very gently so that small bubbles just break the surface. If it boils, it will get cloudy.
- Do not add salt to stock because often stocks are reduced. Season the soup, not the stock.
- When preparing a protein-based stock, add the meat first to the (cold) liquid and bring it to a boil. Skim off the white, and then tan, scum that rises to the surface before adding vegetables and other ingredients such as herbs and spices.
- For tough cuts, such as beef brisket or ham hock, simmer the protein for up to 24 hours before adding the vegetables, which will impart all their flavor and body to the stock after 1 to 2 hours.
- To remove the fat from a stock, strain, preferably into a stainless steel bowl, which allows the stock to cool faster. Once the fat rises to the top, remove it with a ladle or allow the stock to cool to room temperature, then refrigerate it, usually overnight, or until the fat on the surface becomes solid, so that it can be removed easily.
- All stocks freeze well if stored in an airtight container and can be kept frozen up to 3 months.

# BEEF STOCK

BEEF STOCK is the most challenging stock to make because it requires a good number of meaty bones, which are usually expensive, to extract enough flavor and body to make a good stock. Look for meaty rounds of beef shank, resembling giant osso buco, sometimes on special at the meat counter. Freeze until you accumulate enough to make this rich-tasting stock. French onion soup made with real homemade beef stock is like none you've ever had, unless you've eaten it at the old Les Halles market in Paris.

**1.** Place the beef in a large soup pot and cover with water. Bring to a boil, skimming as necessary. Stick the onion with the cloves and add to the pot.

**2.** Add the remaining ingredients, cover, and reduce heat to a bare simmer. Leave to simmer very slowly overnight.

**3.** Strain, discarding the solids (beef bones are too hard for the disposal), cool, and then chill overnight (see Appendix, page 144). The next day, remove and discard the solidified white fat from the top. Freeze, if desired.

# BEAN/CHICKPEA STOCK

WHENEVER YOU COOK DRIED BEANS or other legumes, such as chickpeas and lentils, save the cooking liquid, which will be full of body and flavor. Use it as a base for vegetable and, of course, bean soups.

**Makes about 5 quarts (6 L), serves 15 to 20**

### INGREDIENTS

- 5 pounds (2.3 kg) beef back ribs, beef shin (on the bone) cut into 1-inch (2.5 cm) cross sections, or other tough but flavorful cut of beef, such as brisket or chuck, preferably on the bone
- 1 onion, unpeeled
- 3 to 4 whole cloves
- 2 carrots
- 3 bay leaves
- 2 to 3 leeks, white and light green parts
- 1 teaspoon (2 g) coriander seeds
- 1 teaspoon (2 g) black peppercorns

# SOUPMAKER'S TIP

### SAVING BEEF SCRAPS:

Because beef stock is generally the most expensive stock to make, with the exception of veal or lobster stock, it is well worth the time and effort it takes to save, wrap, and freeze all beef trimmings—include some fat, but cut off any large chunks. After you accumulate enough trimmings (at least 2 to 3 pounds, or 1 to 1.5 kg), defrost the trimmings, roast at 400°F (200°C, or gas mark 6) until deep brown, and add to the stock pot. Supplement with purchased beef bones and trimmings as needed.

# CHICKEN STOCK, TURKEY STOCK

SAVE ROASTED CHICKEN or turkey carcasses, chicken wing tips, backbones, and other trimmings and supplement as needed with inexpensive chicken legs and thighs or backs and necks. I like to use inexpensive turkey wings to fortify this stock. With their high content of gelatin-producing collagen, they add body and a rich flavor. After cooling the stock, ladle it into plastic 1-quart (1 L) containers (or even freezer bags, sealed carefully) and freeze. Frozen stock just needs a minute or two in the microwave to melt enough so that it slides right out of the bag into a pot, ready to boil.

**1.** In a large stockpot, combine the chicken parts (and turkey winfs, if using) with 1 gallon (4 L) cold water. Bring to a boil, skimming off and discarding the white foam impurities that rise to the surface. Continue to simmer until the foam turns light brown and skim that away as well.

**2.** Add the remaining ingredients and bring to a boil again, skimming as necessary. Reduce the heat to a bare simmer and cook, partially covered, for 6 hours, or until the chicken meat falls easily off the bones. Strain through a sieve or china cap into a large, stainless steel bowl or another pot, discarding the solids.

**3.** In hot weather, place the strained stock into a sink full of ice mixed with water and cool for about 1 hour. In cool weather, cool at room temperature. Refrigerate overnight. The next day, remove and discard any fat from the surface. If desired, freeze the stock at this point.

**Makes 1 gallon (4 L), serves 12 to 16**

### INGREDIENTS

- 5 pounds (2.3 kg) mixed chicken parts (necks, backs, wings, and legs), preferably from grain-fed chickens, defrosted if frozen, rinsed and drained
- 1 pound (455 g) turkey wings, optional (to add extra collagen, which lends rich, slightly sticky mouthful to the stock)
- 1 onion, unpeeled but with any moldy or spoiled skin removed and discarded
- 2 carrots, peeled or carrot tops and tails (but not peelings, which will make the stock bitter)
- 2 ribs celery and/or celery root trimmings
- 3 bay leaves
- 1 teaspoon (1.8 g) coriander seeds
- 1 teaspoon (2 g) fennel seeds
- 1 teaspoon (1.7 g) peppercorns
- A small handful of tender herb trimmings (parsley, dill, tarragon, thyme)

## SOUPMAKER'S TIP

**ROASTED CHICKEN OR TURKEY STOCK:**
Never discard the carcass of a roasted chicken or turkey. If you're not ready to cook it at the time, simply wrap in plastic and freeze it. A roasted stock (or brown stock, as opposed to white stock in French cuisine) works best for gravies and sauces; a white stock, made from uncooked bones and trimmings, works best for soups. But there is no law (at least in America) that says you can't mix them.

# CORNCOB STOCK

THIS SWEET, GOLDEN BROTH can be used to add flavor to soups, risotto with corn, or any recipe calling for vegetable stock. You'll be surprised at how much flavor the bare cobs will impart to the stock, so save and freeze corncobs anytime you cut the kernels off of them. For this stock, you can also add tomato trimmings and/or basil sprigs and stems, if desired.

**Makes about 1 gallon (4 L), serves 8 to 12**

### INGREDIENTS

- 12 corncobs kernels cut off (see Appendix, page 144) and reserved for another use, such as the Corn Cream Soup with Summer Vegetables, page 58)
- 2 teaspoons (3.4 g) black and/or white peppercorns
- A handful each of parsley, thyme, and/or tarragon stems
- 4 bay leaves

**1.** Combine corncobs and remaining ingredients in a large soup pot.

**2.** Add about 1 gallon (4 L) cold water, or enough water to cover the cobs by about 3 inches (7.5 cm).

**3.** Bring to a boil, skimming as necessary. Reduce the heat to a slow simmer and cook 1 hour or until the broth is full of corn flavor.

**4.** Pick out the cobs using tongs, a cook's fork, or slotted spoon and discard.

**5.** Strain the remainder of the stock. Discard the solids in a trash bag rather than the garbage disposal.

**6.** Pour the strained stock into smaller containers but always leave the last ½ cup (120 ml) or so of liquid behind and discard it, as this contains the dregs—the scum, or impurities—which sink to the bottom.

**7.** Cool and then refrigerate or divide into quart (liter) or other containers and freeze until ready to use, up to 3 months. (Be sure to label and date the containers; you know what's in those containers now but likely won't in 2 months when they're buried in the depths of the freezer.)

# SMOKED PORK OR TURKEY STOCK

USE EITHER SMOKED PORK BONES, including inexpensive but meaty and flavorful neck bones, or smoked turkey wings or legs to make this rich-tasting, smoky stock perfectly suited to hearty bean soups. Look for pork neck bones in markets that cater to a Southern and/or African American clientele for the best smoky stock ever. Smoked turkey legs, neck bones, wings, or tails all work well.

### Makes about 1 gallon (4 L), serves 12 to 16

**INGREDIENTS**

- 5 pounds (2.3 kg) smoked pork bones (or smoked turkey wings and/or legs)
- 1 large unpeeled onion, cut into rough chunks
- 3 to 4 carrots, cut into rough chunks
- 3 to 4 ribs celery, cut into rough slices
- 1 bay leaf
- 2 sprigs fresh thyme

**1.** Place all the ingredients into a large soup or stock pot. Add 5 quarts (5 L) cold water—1 quart (1 L) for every pound of bones. Bring to a boil, and then reduce the heat to a bare simmer, skimming to remove any white foam that rises to the top. Simmer about 6 hours, or until the bones are soft enough to fall apart completely.

**2.** Cool slightly and then strain, discarding the solids. Refrigerate overnight. The next day, remove and discard any solid fat congealed on the top, and then use or freeze.

# SHRIMP STOCK

IF YOU'RE A SHRIMP LOVER, be sure to save all the shells when peeling shrimp. Freeze in a tightly sealed container or ziplock freezer bag. When you have accumulated at least 3 quarts (3 L), rinse under cold water and use to make this shrimp stock. (The shells from other crustaceans such as lobster and crayfish may be combined with the shrimp shells.)

### Makes about 1 gallon (4 L), serves 12 to 16

**INGREDIENTS**

- 3 quarts (3 L) shrimp shells
- 1 cup (235 ml) dry white vermouth
- 1 tablespoon (6 g) pickling spice
- 1 tablespoon (5 g) coriander seeds
- 1 tablespoon (5.8 g) fennel seeds
- 4 bay leaves
- 4 sprigs fresh thyme, or 1 teaspoon dried thyme
- 1 teaspoon (2 g) crushed black pepper
- 2 lemons, cut in half

In a large pot, combine the shrimp shells, 1 gallon (4 L) cold water, the vermouth, pickling spice, coriander and fennel seeds, bay leaves, thyme, pepper, the juice squeezed from the lemons, and the lemon halves. Bring to a boil, skimming as necessary, and then reduce the heat and simmer for 30 minutes. Strain and cool (see Appendix, page 144). You may freeze any extra stock once it reaches room temperature.

# FISH STOCK

FISH STOCK IS QUICK AND EASY to make; it's ready in about 1 hour. The only challenge is getting good, sweet, briny-smelling fish "frames": skeletons left after removing the fillets; heads, rich in flavor and gelatin (but remove the bitter tasting sharp gills either with a pair of pliers or with your hands wrapped in a towel, or ask the fishmonger to remove them); or simply use fish trimmings. Make friends with your fishmonger; he or she will usually give you the bones for free and may even clean them if you ask nicely (and buy fish regularly). Use the stock for the New England–Style Clam Chowder (page 128), the Alaska Wild Salmon Chowder with Bacon, Leeks, and Dill (page 126), the Scallop and White Corn Chowder with Roasted Poblano Chiles (page 124), and others.

1. Rinse the fish bones and heads in cold water. Place them in a large stock pot with the remaining ingredients. Add 1 gallon (4 L) of cold water and bring to a boil. Skim as necessary and reduce the heat to a bare simmer. Cook slowly for 35 to 40 minutes.

2. Strain the liquid and chill, removing any solidified fat (see Appendix, page 144). The stock called *fumet* in French, will not keep beyond 3 to 5 days.

3. Place in a tightly sealed container and freeze for up to 1 month, defrosting when needed.

**Makes about 1 gallon (4 L), serves 12 to 16**

**INGREDIENTS**

- 5 pounds (2.3 kg) fish bones (clean and sweet-smelling)
- 2 cups (473 ml) dry white wine (substitute or combine with dry white vermouth)
- 2 ribs celery
- 1 onion peeled and cut into large pieces
- 2–3 sprigs fresh thyme, dill, or tarragon
- 1 bay leaf
- 10 crushed peppercorns
- 1 lemon, cut in half

# SOUPMAKER'S TIP

**DIFFERENT FISH MAKE DIFFERENT STOCKS:** One of the subtleties of fish cookery is that different fish make different stocks. Flat fish such as flounder and halibut make the gelatinous stocks, rich in body with delicate flavor. Red Snapper makes a superb light, clear, flavorful stock. Oily fish such as salmon or bluefish are generally too strong in flavor for stock, though salmon stock may be used as the base for a salmon chowder such as the Alaska Wild Salmon Chowder with Bacon, Leeks, and Dill on page 126.

# MUSHROOM STOCK

USE THIS STOCK WHEN you want an earthy mushroom flavor, or use as an alternative vegetarian stock when you want a heartier, more robust flavor. It is perfect for a vegetarian version of mushroom soup (see page 66). Save any mushroom trimmings and stems in the freezer to use here. Shiitake stems are especially full of flavor and too tough and woody to use easily for other purposes. If using portobello stems, cut away and discard the lower portion, which often contains bits of mushroom-growing soil. In addition, use limited quantities of portobello stems, as these will yield a very dark stock.

**Makes about 1 gallon (4 L), serves 12 to 16**

**INGREDIENTS**

- ½ cup (5 g) dried porcini mushroom (or dried shiitakes)
- 3 pounds (1.4 kg) sliced mushrooms or mushroom trimmings
- 1 cup (235 ml) dry white vermouth or white wine
- 1 tablespoon (5.8 g) fennel seed
- 1 teaspoon (1.7 g) black peppercorns
- 5 to 6 sprigs thyme, or substitute 1 teaspoon (1 g) dried thyme
- 4 bay leaves

**1.** Reconstitute the dried porcini mushrooms using 2 cups (475 ml) of water (see "Using Dried Porcini Mushrooms," page 68).

**2.** In a large soup pot, combine the soaked porcini, strained mushroom liquor, mushrooms, vermouth, fennel seeds, peppercorns, thyme, and bay leaves. Cover with 1 gallon (4 L) of water and bring to a boil, skimming as necessary. Simmer about 2 hours

**3.** Strain out the solids, pressing well to extract all the liquid, and cool.

# VEGETABLE STOCK

THERE IS NO ONE RECIPE for making vegetable stock, but this one is a good basic. A vegetable stock will never have the rich body of one made with meat because the vegetables do not contain collagen. For a vegetable substitute, use the liquid drained from cooking chickpeas, or drained from a can of chickpeas. It is particularly rich in soluble fiber, or pectin, which mimics the body of meat-based stocks. Vegetable stock is rather perishable, so use or freeze it within 3 days.

**Makes about 3 quarts (3 L)**

## INGREDIENTS

3 quarts, about 6 pounds (2.7 kg) assorted vegetable trimmings including any or all of the following:

| | |
|---|---|
| Asparagus | Use any trimmings, including peelings. |
| Bay leaves | Add 3 to 4 sweet, mild Mediterranean bay laurel leaves; avoid California bay, which is acrid and overly strong. |
| Beets | Use 1 red beet for stock that will benefit from rosy color, such as stock to be used for tomato or red lentil soup. Use 1 golden beet for any stock to impart sweet flavor and gold color. |
| Black peppercorns and coriander seeds | Add about 1 tablespoon (5 g) each; fennel seed is another good addition. |
| Carrots | Use the tips and root ends. Do not use peels, which are too bitter. |
| Celery | Use the tips, trimmings, and leaves; don't overdo the celery leaves or the stock will be bitter. |
| Celery root | Soak parings in cold water to remove any dirt among the rootlets. Adds fantastic flavor. |
| Corncobs | These can successfully be frozen and add lots of sweet corn flavor. |
| Fennel | Use light-colored stalks, root trimmings, and tough outer layer; keep the darker green stalks for another use (such as chopped fine, and then processed and mixed into tuna or salmon salad or cakes). |
| Green beans | Use the tips and trimmings. |
| Mushrooms | Stems from shiitakes, cremini, and portobellos are especially flavorful. Avoid using dark open mushroom caps, especially those of portobellos, which will dye the stock an unpleasant color. |
| Pea pods | Full of sweet flavor, they're used traditionally to make Venetian *risi e bisi* (soupy rice and peas). |
| Potatoes | Use the trimmings and a few peelings, especially if using thin-skinned potatoes. |
| Scallions | Use the white root ends, not the green tips. |
| Squash | Use the trimmings and parings from hard squash such as butternut or calabaza. |
| Sweet potato | Trimmings from white and/or yellow sweet potatoes (also known as yams) add sweet flavor and golden color to vegetable stock. |
| Sweet red, yellow, or orange bell pepper | Use the trimmings and stems, including seed portion in the center. |
| Tender herb trimmings and stems | Use herbs such as parsley, thyme, basil, marjoram, chives, lovage, tarragon, chervil, and dill. Strong, resinous herbs such as rosemary, oregano, savory, and sage are too strong for stock. |
| Tomatoes | Use the trimmings, cores, seeds, and skins of plum tomatoes. (I don't peel round tomatoes because their thin skins disappear when cooked.) |
| Yellow or white onion | Use peels and trimmings. Onions with several layers of yellow skin will impart a dark golden color to your stock, so keep these for darker roasted chicken or beef stock, and use light-colored onion skins for light stocks such as fish or chicken. |
| Zucchini and/or yellow squash | All trimmings work well in vegetable stock, imparting light vegetable flavor. |

## SOUPMAKER'S TIPS

- Do not use red cabbage and red onions for stock (these will bleed an unpleasant dark gray color). Also, do not use dark green vegetables such as artichoke trimmings, green scallion tops, and the outer layers of leeks (these will be overly dark in color and will make for a slightly bitter stock). Dark onion skin from older onions will darken vegetable stock too much. Use green herbs (trimmings and/or stems) in smaller quantities—their flavor is good but too much will yield a dark greenish stock from the chlorophyll they contain.

- Don't put stringy stock vegetables into the disposal (especially celery, herb stems, and fennel stalks), as they will tend to burn out the motor. You may pick those out and grind the remainder. Chicken bones, other than the large leg bones, will usually grind successfully in the disposal, as will smaller fish bones.

- Freeze trimmings; ideally, use a vacuum-seal method, which is the best way to prevent freezer burn. If that is not possible, place in a plastic ziplock bag and squeeze out as much air as possible. Before using, dump frozen trimmings into a large bowl of water and rinse to remove freezer frost, which carries unpleasant odors.

**1.** Combine all the vegetable trimmings in a large stockpot and cover with about 1 gallon (4 L) of cold water.

**2.** Bring to a boil, reduce heat, and skim as necessary.

**3.** Simmer for 1 hour or until the vegetables are quite soft.

**4.** Strain into a large, deep bowl and cool.

**5.** The finished vegetable stock should be clear with a light golden color, not cloudy or greenish. Transfer to smaller containers for freezing, leaving the dregs that fall to the bottom behind. You may freeze the stock once it reaches room temperature.

See Appendix, page 144.

# COURT BOUILLON

COURT BOUILLON, literally "short [cooking] broth," compared with a rich and complex slow-cooked stock. Rather than the gelatin-rich bones used to make most traditional stocks, court bouillon is usually made with acidic ingredients such as lemon juice, wine, or vinegar to help extract flavors from the vegetable aromatics in the broth, and it is ready in about 1 hour. Court bouillon is often used to poach seafood. The strained liquid can then be used as seafood stock for seafood stews and chowders. Unlike stock, salt is added to court bouillon, because it is not usually reduced, which would concentrate the liquid and make it overly salty.

In a large pot, combine the water, wine, pickling spice, red pepper flakes, salt, the juice squeezed from the lemons and the lemon halves, the onion, celery, garlic, peppercorns, thyme, and bay leaves. Bring to a boil, reduce the heat to a simmer, and cook 30 minutes; then strain, discarding the solids. Use immediately or cool and chill in the refrigerator for up to 4 days before using. If desired, freeze for up to 1 month before using.

**Makes about 1 gallon (4 L), serves 12 to 16**

**INGREDIENTS**

- 1 gallon (4 L) cold water
- 2 cups (473 ml) dry white wine or dry white vermouth
- 2 tablespoons (12 g) pickling spice
- 1 tablespoon (3.6 g) hot red pepper flakes
- 1 teaspoon sea salt
- 2 lemons, cut in half
- 1 onion, chopped
- 1 celery rib, chopped
- 1 garlic clove, smashed
- 1 teaspoon (1.7 g) black peppercorns
- 6 sprigs fresh thyme
- 2 bay leaves

# Chapter 2

# CLEAR BROTH-BASED SOUPS

Clear-based broths are versatile and healthy and so easy to concoct.

THE LIGHTEST OF SOUPS and probably the most challenging to make are clear soups or broths like those in this chapter. Our goal here is cook a broth that is full of flavor but still clear. Cloudiness happens when the protein impurities contained in the liquid coagulate or thicken in small bits. Classic clear bouillons, broths, and consommés may be clarified—traditionally done by adding lightly beaten egg white and crushed egg shells to cold broth heating slowly.

Because clarifying removes flavor as well as the gelatin that lends body to the broth, it's important to include meat, aromatic vegetables, and tomato, which helps draw out the impurities, when clarifying. As the mixture is slowly heated, the protein contained in the egg white and the meat draw any protein impurities together as it coagulates and forms a "raft" that rises to the top while continuing to collect particles from the broth. This raft is then scooped out, strained out, or poured through cheesecloth to obtain a limpid broth.

Chefs in the molecular gastronomy movement have developed an elaborate method of clarifying by freezing stock and allowing it to thaw in a mesh strainer over a bowl at just above the freezing temperature of water. As the liquid melts, the gelatin it contains forms a stable network through cross-linking. The network acts as a filter, trapping large particles of fat or protein, while allowing water and smaller, flavoring compounds to pass through. This method yields a very clear stock though it will not have the rich mouthfeel of gelatin, which traps the impurities and is then filtered out.

In this chapter, we make a simple Roasted Chicken Broth (page 20), and move on to Grandma's Jewish Chicken Soup with Kreplach (page 22), a form of dumpling or ravioli. We also make Sichuan Hot and Sour Soup with Duck, Watercress, and Tofu (page 28) with toasted Sichuan peppercorns. The quickly made Tom Kha Gai (Thai Chicken Coconut Soup) on page 31 is scented with fragrant wild lime leaves and gets its creaminess from using coconut, not dairy products.

The rich Pennsylvania Dutch Chicken Corn Soup with Rivels (page 33) is traditionally made using a rooster or an old stewing hen and includes rivels, a type of small hand-shaped pasta. This soup, which combines New World corn with Old World dumplings, is often served during large summertime community dinners. The South Indian Tomato-Tamarind Rasam (page 36) is a light vegan soup based on the liquid left after cooking split yellow lentils and tart with tamarind purée. The simple Roman Stracciatella (page 40), an egg and cheese drop soup scented with lemon zest and fresh grated nutmeg, can be prepared in about ten minutes if you've got the broth.

# ROASTED CHICKEN BROTH

BROTHS MADE FROM ROASTED MEAT won't give off much foam, making it easier to achieve a richly flavored clear broth. Because the cost of a whole chicken isn't much more than the equivalent amount of chicken breast, it's worthwhile to roast a whole bird and remove the breast to dice and add to the finished broth, to slice for sandwiches, to shred into chicken salad, and so on. Chicken breast cooked on the bone, as here, will be much juicier than boneless, skinless chicken. It is important to roast the chicken in a pan just large enough to hold it to prevent the delicious, collagen-rich pan juices from burning.

1

**Makes about 3 quarts, (3 L), serves 6 to 9**

### INGREDIENTS

- 1 whole roasting chicken, weighing about 5 pounds
- 1 tablespoon (2.4 g) finely chopped fresh thyme leaves, substitute 1 teaspoon (1.4 g) dried thyme
- 2 teaspoons (12.5 g) kosher salt, substitute 1 teaspoon (6 g) table or sea salt
- ¼ teaspoon freshly ground black pepper
- 4 quarts (4 L) cold water
- 1 medium yellow onion, unpeeled, cut into large chunks
- 3 carrots, about ½ pound (225 g), cut into large chunks
- 3 ribs celery, about ¼ pound (115 g), sliced about ½-inch (1 cm) thick

## SOUPMAKER'S TIPS

❊ Include any giblets but not the liver, which would make the broth cloudy. The better the chicken; the better the flavor. grain-fed or pastured chicken is the best choice.

**2**

**5**

**6**

**7**

**1.** Season the chicken with a mixture of fresh thyme, kosher salt, and freshly ground black pepper and and then roast it at high heat. After the chicken cools, cut away the breast meat before making the broth.

**2.** Slide the chicken and any roasting juices from the pan into a large soup pot.

**3.** If the juices stick to the pan, add enough water to cover the bottom of the pan and place it in a moderate oven to melt for about 20 minutes. Use a silicone spatula or wooden spoon (avoid metal) to scrape the melted juices into the pot.

**4.** Add enough water to cover the chicken by about 2 inches (5 cm), about 4 quarts (4 L). Bring to a boil, skimming off any foam impurities, and reduce heat. Simmer 3 hours or until the bones can be easily broken apart.

**5.** Now add the vegetables—here a simple mirepoix of cut-up onion, carrot, and celery—and bring back to a boil.

**6.** Reduce heat and simmer about 3 hours longer or until the chicken breaks apart easily.

**7.** Strain the broth though a china cap or a wire sieve, discarding the solids. (Note that chicken bones may be ground successfully in the garbage disposal but be sure to remove the tough large leg bones first and discard in the trash.) Cool (see Appendix, page 144), and then transfer broth to smaller storage containers, discarding the last 1 inch (2.5 cm) or so of the liquid because it contains the dregs, which fall to the bottom and would make the liquid cloudy.

# GRANDMA'S JEWISH CHICKEN SOUP WITH KREPLACH

GRANDMA WOULD USE an entire pre-salted kosher stewing hen complete with the gelatin-rich feet and she'd leave the golden dots of fat in the bowl when serving for extra richness. In this recipe, we supplement the chicken with inexpensive turkey wings which impart full-bodied flavor and plenty of natural gelatin. (Extra chicken wings or even better, chicken feet—sometimes sold as "chicken paws" will do the same.) A leftover roasted chicken carcass would make a wonderful addition to the pot. The kreplach, thought to be a variation on the word

*crepe*, are the Eastern European (or Ashkenazi) Jewish version of Chinese wonton and Italian ravioli and may have been brought to eastern Europe by traders along the Silk Route from China or from traders bringing goods from Italy. Though sometimes hard to find, root parsley, also known as Hamburg parsley, is a traditional soup vegetable. Substitute celery root for part or all of the celery ribs, if desired. This soup freezes well without the kreplach. Freeze the kreplach separately, preferably uncooked.

**Makes 3 quarts (3 L), serves 8**

### INGREDIENTS

- 1 whole large (about 5 pounds, or 2.3 kg) roaster chicken, or 5 pounds (2.3 kg) chicken backs and necks
- 2 pounds (907 g) turkey wings (optional: include chicken feet and/or chicken wings)
- 3 ribs celery, divided (1 whole and 2 finely diced)
- 2 parsley roots, divided (1 whole and 1 peeled and thinly sliced, or substitute parsnip)
- 3 carrots, divided (1 whole and 2 peeled and thinly sliced)
- 2 leeks, washed thoroughly, divided (1 whole and 1 thinly sliced)
- 1 whole yellow onion
- 2 to 3 large sprigs dill
- 2 bay leaves
- Beef Kreplach (recipe follows)
- 2 tablespoons (7 g) chopped dill, for garnish
- Kosher salt and freshly ground black pepper

Ingredients for nourishing, reviving Jewish Chicken Soup to cure what ails you.

1. Put the chicken parts, turkey wings, (and chicken feet and chicken wings, if desired), along with about 1 gallon (4 L) cold water, enough to cover the chicken by 2 to 3 inches (5 to 7.5 cm) into a large soup pot. Bring to a boil over moderate heat, skimming off any foam. When no more foam rises up, add the whole celery, parsley root, carrot, leek, onion, dill sprigs, and bay leaves. Bring back to a boil and skim as necessary. Reduce heat to a bare simmer, cover with the lid slightly ajar and cook 4 to 6 hours, or up to overnight.

2. Strain out the solids and discard them. Cool the soup and chill overnight in the refrigerator and then remove and discard the solid fat from the top. Alternatively, allow the soup broth to rest so that the fat rises to the top and then skim off and discard as much of the fat as possible. Use a paper towel placed directly onto the soup to mop up more of the fat.

4  5

3. When ready to serve the soup, bring a medium pot of generously salted water to a boil. Add the kreplach and boil 3 to 4 minutes or until the edges (where there is a double layer of dough) are tender and floppy rather than stiff. Drain.

4. Bring the soup to a boil and add the diced celery, sliced parsley root, sliced carrots, sliced leeks, and chopped dill. Bring to a boil, season to taste with salt and black pepper, and add the boiled kreplach.

5. Serve the soup piping hot and enjoy!

# BEEF KREPLACH

**KREPLACH DOUGH:**

**Makes about 1 pound (455 g) dough**

- ¾ pound (3 cups minus 3 tablespoons, or 340 g) all-purpose flour or pastry flower
- 1 teaspoon (6 g) salt
- 3 eggs, beaten
- 3 tablespoons (45 ml) cold water

**Brown-shell eggs, which have thicker shells than white eggs so they stay fresher longer, and unbleached all-purpose or pastry flour make for tender, pliable dough.**

# SOUPMAKER'S TIPS

❋ As the dough is rolled out thinner, it may begin to get sticky, especially on the next-to-last and last rounds. Dust with more flour as needed but don't overdo it. Once you fully roll out the pasta, coat it with a thin to nonexistent layer of flour. Any excess flour that is not incorporated into the dough will wash off in the cooking water and tend to make gluey pasta.

❋ If the dough breaks apart, is irregularly shaped, or sticks to the machine and makes holes, do not worry. Just fold up the sheet of dough into a regular shape that fits the width of the pasta machine. Dust the new sheet of dough with flour, and start rolling again, again following all the steps.

❋ If the dough is elastic and wants to spring back, push back into a compact shape, cover, and allow it to rest at room temperature for about 30 minutes to relax the gluten.

## SAVE FOR STOCK:

Celery and carrot trimmings, leek root sections and any light-colored leaf trimmings (do not use the dark outer leaves, which will be dark and bitter), dill stems, parsley root parings (especially good in chicken and vegetable stocks)—soak the parings in cold water to remove the dirt from in between the rootlets.

2    4

**1.** Measure the flour, preferably by weighing on a digital scale for accuracy. Add the salt and combine.

**2.** Mound the flour in a large bowl to form a flour "volcano" with a "crater" in the middle. Pour the eggs and water into the crater. Using a table fork, begin to incorporate the flour, starting with the inner rim.

**3.** Once you incorporate about half the flour and the mixture has formed a shaggy mass, transfer the dough to a work surface, preferably a wooden board, which has been dusted lightly with flour.

**4.** Begin to knead the dough while incorporating the remaining flour, turning the dough mass over several times while kneading so that the moist side of the dough is exposed to the flour, encouraging the flour to be absorbed.

Use the heel of your palm to push the dough down and away, then fold the edge over top to keep a basically round dough ball. Rotate the dough mass clockwise if you are left handed and counterclockwise if right handed.

Continue kneading the dough about 5 minutes or until the dough is cohesive and moderately smooth. (Running the dough through the pasta sheeter will develop the gluten further, making it smooth and elastic.) The dough should stick lightly to your fingers. Form the dough into a round ball pulling from the outside to the center on the bottom, so the bottom portion joins together in the center and the top is smooth.

Cover the dough with a bowl or a damp cloth, or wrap in plastic and allow it to rest for 30 minutes at room temperature before rolling. The dough will continue to absorb flour as it rests and relaxes.

Meanwhile, prepare the kreplach filling (recipe follows).

### KREPLACH FILLING:

- 2 tablespoons (30 ml) vegetable oil
- 1 small onion, finely chopped
- 1 clove garlic, minced
- ½ pound (225 g) ground beef
- 2 tablespoons (8 g) finely chopped flat-leaf parsley
- 1 egg yolk
- 1 teaspoon (6 g) kosher salt
- ¼ teaspoon black pepper

**1.** Heat the oil in a large skillet; add the onions and garlic, and sauté until well browned. Add the ground beef to the pan and brown on high heat, stirring frequently. Stir in the parsley.

**2.** Transfer the beef mixture to a medium bowl and allow it to cool to room temperature.

**3.** Meanwhile, crack the egg at the widest part of the shell so the shell breaks into two relatively even halves. Allow most of the white to drain out and discard or reserve for another use (egg whites freeze very well).

**4.** Transfer the yolk back and forth from one half of the shell to the other to drain off the remaining white.

**5.** Add the yolk to the cooled beef mixture and thoroughly combine the meat-onion mixture with the egg yolk, salt, and pepper. Cool and then refrigerate filling about 1 hour before using.

### ASSEMBLING THE KREPLACH:

**1.** Cut the dough ball into four sections, keeping all but one covered to prevent the dough from forming a hard skin.

**2.** Using the palm of your hand, flatten out a section of dough by hand.

**3.** Form the dough into a rough "tongue" shape. Dust lightly with flour on both sides. Using a hand-cranked pasta sheeter with the largest opening between the rollers (number 1 or 0), roll out the dough. Close up the opening between the rollers to number 1 or 2 and roll the dough section out again so that it's long and thin.

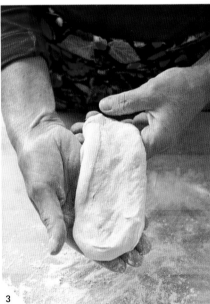

7

8    10

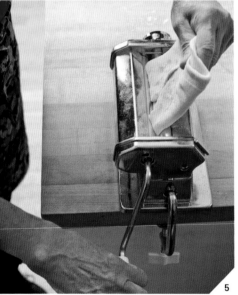

5

**4.** Remove the dough from the machine and fold in thirds lengthwise, dimpling with your fingers so the layers adhere. (The object is to get an even piece of dough almost as wide as the rollers.)

**5.** Place the dough crosswise in the slot of the pasta sheeter. Go back to the largest opening, either 0 or 1 on the pasta sheeter, as the dough is now double-thick.

**6.** Begin feeding the folded dough through the sheeter while cranking smoothly, sprinkling on both sides with flour as needed to prevent sticking.

**7.** Continue to roll, reducing the thickness of the dough one number for each round of rolling until the dough is quite thin but not transpar-

ent, usually the next to last or second to last setting on the machine. Do not skip any numbers as the action of rolling also kneads the dough until it is smooth and elastic.

**8.** Cut the dough sheet into 2 or 3 lengths to make them easier to handle. Trim off the ends to make a straight line.

**9.** To make squares, fold the dough in thirds crosswise to make guide lines.

**10.** Unfold and cut along the guide lines to make 3 fat strips.

**11.** Dust the strips lightly with flour, then place them one on top of the next in an even stack.

**12.** Cut crosswise into square shapes.

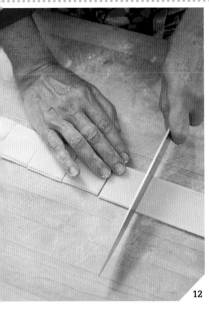

13. Separate into individual pieces, keeping most of the squares covered with a damp kitchen towel so they don't dry out. Have the chilled filling ready.

14. Using your fingertips or a small teaspoon, place 1 generous teaspoon (1 g) of the kreplach filling in the center of each square.

Take care not to get any filling on the edges of the dough because it will prevent the dough from forming a good seal.

15. Pull the far edge of the dough over the filling for each kreplach.

16. Starting at the top point, press the edges together to form a triangle (or half-moon, if using dough circles). Push out the excess air from the open sides and press the edges together firmly to seal. If the edges don't stick together (because the dough is too firm and/or the air in the room is too dry), use your fingertip to brush the edges with a little water before pressing the edges together.

17. Continue filling and shaping the kreplach until all the filling is used, arranging the filled kreplach on a mesh pasta drying rack or a clean cotton cloth sprinkled lightly with flour to prevent sticking.

18. If desired, gather together excess dough, wrap and allow it to rest 30 minutes to relax the gluten, then roll out and cut into thin strips for noodles. Either add to the soup or dry and reserve for another use.

Cover the finished kreplach with a clean, slightly damp towel to keep them from hardening until you're ready to cook them.

# SICHUAN HOT AND SOUR SOUP WITH DUCK, WATERCRESS, AND TOFU

THIS SOUP MAY BRING tears to your eyes and is a reputed cold remedy, especially because it contains abundant chopped fresh ginger root. Served in countless versions in Chinese restaurants across North America and elsewhere, it is usually made with chicken or pork broth seasoned with a mixture of hot chile pepper, earthy, hot ground white pepper, and Chinese black vinegar and lightly thickened with cornstarch.

Common additions include bamboo shoots, toasted sesame oil, wood ear mushrooms, dried daylily buds, and tofu skin. Both the provinces of Beijing and Sichuan claim the soup as a regional specialty though this version comes from Sichuan province. Here we use duck breast and chicken broth (or stock) and we season it with toasted Sichuan peppercorns and dark, umami-rich mushroom soy sauce.

10

**Makes 1 gallon (4 L), serves 12 to 15**

**MARINATED DUCK:**

- ½ pound (225 g) boneless duck breast, skin removed and reserved for another use
- 2 teaspoons (3 g) Sichuan peppercorns
- 1 tablespoon (15 ml) mushroom soy sauce
- 2 tablespoons (30 ml) rice wine, substitute sake dry sherry or Marsala
- 1 tablespoon (6 g) minced fresh ginger
- 1 teaspoon (3 g) minced garlic
- 1 tablespoon (8 g) cornstarch

2 3 4 7

**1.** Place the duck meat (here two Pekin duck breasts with the skin and fat removed) in the freezer for 30 minutes, or until firm but not hard.

**2.** Slice the duck against the grain (crosswise on the breast) into thin slices.

**3.** Meanwhile, heat a small skillet with no oil and add the Sichuan peppercorns. Toast until fragrant, about 2 minutes. Shake out most of the black inner seeds, if present, and discard.

**4.** Cool, then lightly crush the Sichuan peppercorns with a meat mallet or the side of a chef's knife.

**5.** In a medium bowl combine mushroom soy, Sichuan peppercorns, rice wine, ginger, garlic, and cornstarch.

**6.** Add to the duck and toss to coat.

**7.** Cover and refrigerate marinated duck for 1 to 2 hours to absorb the marinade.

**8.** Place the duck with its marinade and 1 cup (235 ml) water in a small pot and bring to a boil, stirring constantly. Cook until the duck is opaque, about 3 minutes. Cool and reserve for soup (recipe follows).

8

# SOUPMAKER'S TIPS

✳ Sichuan peppercorns are small reddish-brown dried fruits of the prickly ash tree that impart a lingering tingly numbness to the mouth. Their lemony aroma accented by a warm and woodsy flavor is in the fruit itself, not the seeds, which are often removed because of their unpleasant, gritty texture. Lower quality Sichuan peppercorns may contains bits of pointy thorns that can be harmful if swallowed, so check and remove if necessary. In Sichuan cuisine, the peppercorns are lightly toasted and crushed before adding them to food, generally at the last moment and often in combination with fiery chiles or chili oil.

**SAVE FOR STOCK:**

Duck trimmings, duck skin (chop or grind and render—cook very slowly—for delicious duck fat, which is great for frying potatoes), ginger trimmings (add to chicken stock), shiitake mushroom stems (for mushroom stock), scallion root ends.

## HOT AND SOUR SOUP:

- ½ pound (225 g) fresh firm tofu, drained on paper towels
- 3 quarts (3 L) Roasted Chicken Broth (see page 20) or Chicken Stock (see page 9)
- ½ pound (225 g) shiitake mushrooms, stems removed and caps thinly sliced
- 2 tablespoons (30 ml) mushroom soy sauce
- ¼ cup (60 ml) rice wine
- 2 teaspoons (10 ml) roasted Japanese sesame oil
- 2 tablespoons (16 g) cornstarch
- Cooked Marinated Duck (recipe page 29)

- ¼ pound (115 g) snow pea pods, trimmed and sliced into thin strips (see Appendix, page 146)
- 1 bunch scallions, sliced on the bias into ½-inch (1 cm) sections
- ¼ cup (60 ml) Chinese black vinegar, substitute balsamic vinegar
- 1 teaspoon (5 ml) Chinese hot chili oil, or to taste
- 1 teaspoon (2 g) ground white pepper
- 1 tablespoon (4 g) chopped cilantro leaves

**1.** Cut tofu first into slices; then, cut slices into batons.

**2.** Cut batons into small, even cubes and reserve.

**3.** Pour the Roasted Chicken Broth into a large soup pot and bring to a boil, skimming as necessary.

**4.** Add the sliced shiitake mushrooms and stir to combine.

**5.** Combine mushroom soy, rice wine, sesame oil, and cornstarch in a small bowl and reserve, using your fingers to mix in the starch that tends to sink to the bottom after a few minutes.

**6.** Pour the cornstarch/soy mixture into the broth and stir to combine. Bring liquid back to a boil, stirring occasionally so the cornstarch is evenly distributed and the soup is lightly thickened.

**7.** Add the reserved cooked duck meat and cooking liquid.

**8.** Add the snow pea julienne and stir to combine.

**9.** Add the reserved tofu, scallions, black vinegar, chili oil, white pepper, and cilantro and stir to combine.

**10.** Serve the soup piping hot in a tureen, as shown, or in large soup bowls.

# TOM KHA GAI (Thai Chicken Coconut Soup)

*TOM KHA* GAI (OR *KAI*), which means "chicken galangal soup," is a spicy Thai and Laotian soup made with coconut milk, galangal, lemongrass, and chicken. The Laotian version uses dill; the Thai version uses cilantro and Thai basil. Look for the richest (thickest) coconut milk, sometimes known as coconut cream, and make sure it's the unsweetened type (the sweetened type is used for cocktails). This quick-cooking soup is easy to make once you've gathered the ingredients. If you find fresh lime leaves at a Thai grocery, buy extra and freeze them (freezing darkens the color but retains the flavor). This soup does not freeze well.

**Makes 3 quarts (3 L), serves 8 to 12**

### INGREDIENTS

- 1 stalk fresh lemongrass
- 1 Thai green chile pepper, very thinly sliced (or substitute serrano or other small, hot green chile), plus extra for garnish
- 2 cans (14 ounces, or 425 ml) unsweetened coconut milk
- 1 quart (1 L) Chicken Stock (page 9)
- 2 tablespoons (12 g) minced fresh galangal (substitute 2 teaspoons, or 2 g, dried galangal or 2 tablespoons, or 12 g, fresh ginger)
- 8 wild lime leaves (also known as kaffir lime)
- ¾ pound (340 g) boneless, skinless chicken breast, thinly sliced
- ¼ pound (115 g) shiitake mushroom caps, thinly sliced (optional)
- ¼ cup (60 ml) Thai fish sauce (*nam pla*)
- 2 tablespoons (15 g) light brown sugar
- ½ cup (120 ml) fresh squeezed lime juice
- 1 tablespoon (15 ml) Sriracha sauce
- Kosher salt
- 2 tablespoons (8 g) shredded cilantro and/or Thai basil

**Ingredients for Tom Kha Gai**

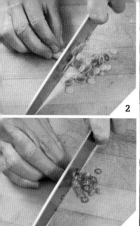

1. Remove and discard the outer woody outer layers of the lemongrass.

2. Thinly slice the tender, inner layers of the lemongrass, which are pink.

3. After handling fresh chiles, take care not to touch tender body parts with your fingers. (For protection, you may want to wear gloves when slicing chiles.)

4. Combine the lemongrass, coconut milk, Chicken Stock, galangal (here dried galangal), and lime leaves in a medium pot and bring to a boil. Simmer 20 minutes, partially covered. Strain out solids and pour broth back into the same pot.

5. Add the chicken breast, shiitake mushrooms (optional), fish sauce, and brown sugar.

Simmer the soup mixture 3 to 5 minutes, stirring, until the chicken is opaque and just cooked through, and then remove from the heat. Add the lime juice and Sriracha sauce and stir to combine. Season to taste with salt.

6. Sprinkle each portion with cilantro leaves and/or Thai basil and a few slices of Thai green chile peppers and serve.

# SOUPMAKER'S TIPS

**Special Thai Ingredients:** Galangal, a rhizome (swollen underground root) related to ginger, consists of reddish-tan cylindrical sections divided by tougher reddish-brown rings and a fibrous interior. Warm, sweet, and spicy, galangal's flavor is reminiscent of cinnamon, ginger, and pine. Ginger is the best substitute. Fresh, frozen, or dried galangal are available at many Asian markets.

✳ Fish sauce is the umami-rich liquid drained off after fermenting small fish with sea salt with a pronounced aroma. This thin, amber sauce is a staple in southeast Asian coastal cuisine.

✳ Wild lime leaves, often called "kaffir," are the perfumed leaves of a southeast Asian citrus fruit. The glossy, grass-green leaves resemble two leaves joined end to end and slightly twisted. Look for fresh wild lime leaves at Southeast Asian markets. Frozen leaves will have all the perfume of the fresh product but with darker color.

✳ Coconut milk is the rich, creamy liquid derived from soaking the grated meat of a mature coconut in water; coconut water is the liquid from a young coconut. Coconut milk has half the fat content of heavy cream. The fat will often rise to the top of the can, so shake well before opening.

**SAVE FOR STOCK:**
Ginger skin, extra lime leaves, chicken breast trimmings, shiitake mushroom stems (Shiitake stems are packed with smoky mushroom flavor. Trim off the ends and add to mushroom stock.)

# PENNSYLVANIA DUTCH CHICKEN CORN SOUP WITH RIVELS

THIS SOUP IS TRADITIONALLY made using rooster, which is difficult to find in the United States, unless you live on a farm or know someone who does. Though tough, the bird will impart deep, intense flavor to the soup. In its absence, we use Chicken Stock in place of water to poach a roasting chicken. Saffron, widely grown in Pennsylvania Dutch country, imparts its golden color, pungent, bittersweet flavor and haylike aroma to the soup. Add a goodly amount of sweet corn and corn broth, simple hand-rolled egg noodles (or you can substitute purchased egg noodles), and you've got a satisfying meal in a bowl. You may enrich the soup by sprinkling it with chopped hard-cooked eggs just before serving.

**Makes 1 gallon (4 L), serves 8 to 12**

### INGREDIENTS

- 2 quarts (2 L) Chicken Stock (page 9)
- 2 quarts (2 L) Corncob Stock (page 10)
- 1 large whole chicken, 4 to 5 pounds (2.3 kg), preferably a large stewing or roasting hen or capon
- 1 large carrot
- 2 ribs celery
- 1 large onion stuck with 4 whole cloves (see Appendix, page 148)
- 4 sprigs lovage, or substitute flat-leaf parsley
- ½ lemon
- 1 pound (455 g) boneless, skinless chicken breast
- 8 ears of fresh corn
- ½ teaspoon saffron threads
- ¾ cup inner stalks celery and leaves, chopped
- Salt and freshly ground pepper
- ½ pound (225 g) or so Rivels (recipe follows)
- ¼ cup (15 g) chopped flat-leaf parsley

Pennsylvannia Dutch Chicken Corn Soup with Rivels is infused with leaves of the old-fashioned herb, lovage, which looks and tastes like extra-large celery leaves on long, hollow stalks and is known as *mountain celery* in many languages.

Return the stock to the pot, add the chicken breasts and poach at a low simmer until the chicken is firm and cooked through, about 10 minutes. Remove the chicken breasts from the broth, allow them to cool, and then cut into small dice.

Meanwhile, cut the kernels from the ears of corn (see Appendix, page 145). It is important to get the most "milk" from the corn, so cut the corn with a sharp knife (not too close to the cob) and go back over the cob with the flat of the knife to release the "milk."

In a large soup pot, bring the Chicken and Corncob Stocks to a boil. Add the whole chicken including any giblets but not the liver, which makes for a cloudy broth. Bring the liquid, which should cover the chicken by about 2 inches (5 cm), back to a boil, skimming as needed to obtain a clear broth. Reduce the heat to low and simmer 2 hours.

**1.** Add the vegetables, onion stuck with cloves, lovage, and lemon and bring back to a boil.

**2.** Reduce heat and simmer slowly 30 minutes longer or until the chicken is very tender. The broth should never boil, because it will become cloudy.

**3.** Remove most of the chicken from the broth using tongs or a slotted spoon to make the broth easier to strain.

**4.** When ready the chicken should fall away easily from the bones. At this point the chicken has lost its nutrients and most of its flavor and may be discarded, though you may use it for chicken salad, croquettes, or other highly-seasoned recipe if desired.

**5.** Strain the broth, discarding the contents of the strainer.

**6.** Allow the broth to settle about 10 minutes and then skim off and discard as much of the fat floating on top as possible, using a ladle or cook's spoon.

Add the corn, saffron, and chopped celery to the broth and simmer until the celery is tender, about 8 minutes. Season to taste with salt and pepper.

**7.** Add the Rivels, dropping them into the liquid one at a time so they don't stick together and boil until tender, 3 to 5 minutes. For a clearer soup, boil the Rivels separately in salted water. Drain and add to the soup just before serving.

**8.** At the last minute, stir in the chopped parsley and serve.

# RIVELS

Rivels are small bits or strands of fresh egg noodle dough formed by hand of German origin. They are essential for traditional Pennsylvania Dutch chicken corn soup.

**Makes about ½ pound (225 g)**

### INGREDIENTS

- 6 ounces (170 g) unbleached all-purpose flour
- Pinch salt
- 1 large egg
- 1 egg yolk
- 1 tablespoon (15 ml) water

**1.** Sift the flour into a bowl with the salt.

**2.** Whisk the egg, yolk, and water together.

**3.** Make a well in the center. Pour egg mixture into the well and mix with a fork to incorporate the flour.

**4.** Continue mixing to incorporate all the flour, beating in a clockwise direction if you're right handed and counterclockwise if you're left handed. A stiff dough should form.

The dough will soften considerably as it rests and hydrates—absorbs the liquid. Wrap the dough in plastic film or cover with a damp towel and allow it to rest at room temperature for about 30 minutes before proceeding.

**5.** Break off small pieces of dough and dip into flour. Shape in your hand into small, rough stringlike lengths.

**6.** Using the palms of your hands, smoothly roll one strip at a time from the center toward the outside edges using light, even pressure, as if you were working with modeling clay.

**7.** Continue rolling the strips, dusting them with flour before dropping into a loose pile. Once all the strips have been rolled out, pick up the pile of strips, dust once more with flour, and shake so they are all coated. Spread the strips onto a flour-dusted baking pan or clean cloth to dry the rivels for use later. Or, shake off any loose flour and drop the rivels into the soup as soon as they are completed.

**SAVE FOR STOCK:**
Onion, carrot, celery trimmings; lovage and parsley stems; and corncobs. Avoid adding a large quantity of parsley stems to your stock as they contain a high proportion of chlorophyll, which will make for an overly dark, slightly bitter stock.

# SOUTH INDIAN TOMATO-TAMARIND RASAM

RASAM, A LIGHT SOUP from southern India, is flavored with tart tamarind pulp, tomato, chile pepper, pepper, cumin, and other spices combined in a mixture known as Rasam powder, which may also be purchased. The liquid from cooking split yellow lentils (or *tuvar dal*) is the soup base. The cooked dal is strained out and reserved for another use, such as seasoned dal over rice or lentil cakes. Rasam, which means "juice" in Sanskrit, is traditionally prepared with black pepper and tamarind, both native to and abundant in southern India. Rasam is the basis of the Anglo-Indian Mulligatawny soup, a corrupted version of two Tamil words meaning "pepper water." Curry leaves—which are available fresh at Indian markets or dried, though with far less of their unique nutty fragrance—are essential. Rasam is often served over a scoop of cooked Basmati rice to make a more substantial dish. This soup is vegan. It freezes very well.

**Makes 3 quarts (3 L), serves 8 to 12**

### INGREDIENTS

- 1 pound (455 g) tuvar dal, also known as split yellow lentils or split pigeon peas
- 2 quarts (2 L) water, divided
- 1 tablespoon (15 ml) vegetable oil
- 2 tablespoons (22 g) black mustard seeds
- 3 sprigs curry leaves, leaves pulled from their stalks
- ½ teaspoon asafetida, optional
- 6 large red ripe tomatoes, diced
- 1 tablespoon (15 g) Rasam Powder (see "Making Rasam Powder [or Rasam Podi," page 38])
- 1 teaspoon (2.2 g) turmeric
- ¼ pound (115 g) tamarind pulp, makes about ½ cup (120 ml) strained pulp (see "Making Tamarind Purée," page 39)
- 2 tablespoons (15 g) dark brown sugar
- Salt
- ½ cup (40 g) grated fresh or frozen coconut, for garnish
- Cilantro, for garnish

1   2

3   6

Combine the dal with 6 cups (1.5 L) water in a medium soup pot. Bring to a boil, reduce heat, cover partially, and simmer until tender, about 30 minutes.

**1.** Meanwhile, heat the oil in a small skillet and add mustard seeds. Cover and cook over moderate heat, shaking the pan, until the mustard seeds begin to pop, about 2 minutes. Continue to cook until the seeds finish popping, about 1 minute longer.

**2.** Uncover, add the curry leaves and asafetida and cook briefly together until fragrant, about 30 seconds. Reserve the contents of the pan.

**3.** Strain dal through a sieve or china cap.

**4.** Reserve the liquid for the soup and reserve the cooked lentils for another use.

**5.** Pour the cooking liquid back into the pot. Add the curry leaf mixture, tomatoes, Rasam Powder, turmeric, and about ¼ cup (60 ml) of the strained tamarind pulp—more if you prefer a more tart flavor. Add the dark brown sugar and season to taste with salt; stir to combine.

**6.** Garnish each portion with grated coconut and cilantro just before serving.

**7.** Serve the soup immediately.

# SOUPMAKER'S TIPS

❊ Look for frozen grated coconut in Asian and Latin American markets. It's as close as possible to fresh without the work!

❊ Asafetida is an intriguing spice that lends a deep savory, or umami, note to many Indian vegetarian legume dishes. Its name translates in many languages to "devil's dung" because of its potent, even stinking, aroma. The dried yellow-brownish resin is extracted from the root of the plant, which is in the fennel and parsley family and grows wild from Central Asia to the eastern coast of the Mediterranean Sea. The pure resin is the strongest; next is gray *hing*—its common name in Indian markets. The mildest version is yellow, which has been mixed with turmeric and other ingredients including wheat flour. Definitely an acquired taste, but once you learn to love it, there is no substitute. A little goes a long way.

❊ Native to tropical India, curry leaves (bottom left and right), are small oval leaves in the citrus family with an earthy, nutty aroma hinting of tangerine and anise. The leaflets, which are dark green on top and pale underneath, run in pairs up the smaller branches of the curry tree and give off a strong, warm aroma when bruised or rubbed. They are essential to the vegetarian cuisine of southern India and Sri Lanka. Curry leaves quickly lose their fragrance when dried so they are used fresh (or frozen) but will last for 1 to 2 weeks refrigerated. Look for fresh, perky, shiny fresh curry leaves or frozen curry leaves in Indian groceries.

TECHNIQUE

# Making Rasam Powder (or Rasam Podi)

This south Indian spice mix is essential for South Indian Tomato-Tamarind Rasam. Try using it to season grilled fish, chicken, or vegetables or sprinkle over cooked rice or legumes. Do not grind the powder finely; it should be rather grainy. Store the Rasam Powder in a tightly sealed container at room temperature for a month or frozen for up to 6 months.

**Makes about 1½ cups (151 g)**

**INGREDIENTS**

- ¾ cup (60 g) coriander seeds
- 1 tablespoon (6 g) cumin seeds
- 1 tablespoon (5 g) black peppercorns
- 1 teaspoon (3.5 g) fenugreek seeds
- 4 whole cloves
- 1 teaspoon (2.5 g) ground cinnamon (preferably true cinnamon from Sri Lanka—see "Soupmaker's Tips")
- 2 tablespoons (7 g) hot red pepper flakes (or other ground hot red chile)
- ¼ cup (28 g) bright red paprika

1

**1.** Combine the coriander, cumin, peppercorns, fenugreek, and cloves in a small skillet and toast over moderate heat until fragrant, about 3 minutes.

2

**2.** Cool, combine with remaining ingredients and grind in a spice grinder or coffee mill to a fine powder. Transfer to an airtight container for storage.

## SOUPMAKER'S TIPS

❊ True cinnamon is the sweetly scented inner bark of the cinnamon tree. Its flavor is warm and spicy yet sweet and delicate and blends well with other spices. Also known as soft-stick cinnamon, true cinnamon sticks will be friable enough to be easily crushed by hand. Cassia, sold as cinnamon in North America, and usually from Indonesia, Vietnam, or China, is thicker and dark reddish brown with a much more potent bold, peppery flavor. Cassia sticks are rolled from the two outer sides toward the center; true cinnamon is up like a rug. Look for true cinnamon sticks and ground powder in specialty spice stores or southern Indian markets (see Resources, page 154).

**SAVE FOR STOCK:**

Tomato trimmings, extra curry leaves

# Making Tamarind Purée

Tamarind pods are brittle and are filled with hard brown seeds surrounded by tangy, stringy edible pulp with a lemony prune flavor. Fresh tamarind pods are available in season in Latin American, Indian, and Asian markets, but the fruit is usually purchased in the form of a dense block of pulp with or without its large hard brown seeds—preferably without. Frozen tamarind purée may be found in Latin American markets and is easy to use. Salted tamarind concentrate may be found in small jars in Indian and sometimes Asian markets. It is more concentrated and salty, so use about half as much as strained tamarind pulp and cut down on salt in any recipe. Reserve remaining tamarind pulp for another use—it freezes well.

Curved brown fresh tamarind pods with dense, gooey inner pulp

**1.** To prepare block tamarind, cut or tear off a piece of the block and soak in warm water to cover about 30 minutes or until the pulp is soft enough to break apart with your hands. If using fresh tamarind, break open the pods, scrape out the pulp, and then soak about 30 minutes.

**2.** Force the soft pulp through a sieve using your hands as shown, or force through a food mill, discarding any seeds and fibers.

**3.** Be sure to scrape off the pulp sticking to the back of the sieve. Store tamarind purée refrigerated for up to 2 weeks or freeze for longer storage.

# ROMAN STRACCIATELLA
## (Egg and Cheese Drop Soup)

STRACCIATELLA—from the Italian *stracciato*, meaning "torn apart" as in rags—is an Italian egg-drop soup usually said to be *alla Romana* (in the style of Rome). It is prepared by beating eggs, adding grated parmesan cheese, salt, pepper, nutmeg, and sometimes semolina, and then adding this mixture to boiling broth. The broth is set whirling first with a whisk, and the beaten egg mixture is added in a slow stream to produce the *stracciatelle* (little shreds) of cooked egg in the broth, which is clarified by the process. In Italy, stracciatella also refers to vanilla gelato with chocolate shavings or to strands of fresh mozzarella that have been pulled apart and mixed with fresh cream and used to stuff burrata, especially in the Murgia region of Puglia.

**Makes 3 quarts (3 L), serves 8 to 12**

### INGREDIENTS

- 1 lemon
- 3 quarts (3 L) Roasted Chicken Broth or rich Beef Stock (page 20 or 8), divided
- 6 tablespoons (89 ml) semolina
- 6 tablespoons (30 g) grated Parmigiano-Reggiano
- ¼ cup (15 g) chopped Italian parsley
- ¼ cup (10 g) chopped fresh basil leaves
- Pinch freshly grated nutmeg
- 6 large eggs
- 2 cups (40 g) lightly packed spinach leaves, cut in thin strips
- Salt and pepper

**SAVE FOR STOCK:**

Egg shells (use to help clarify clear broth), Parmigiano-Reggiano rind (add to vegetable soup such as minestrone or Acquacotta Maremmana, page 83, to flavor the broth—or grill them and serve with drinks), parsley and basil stems, peeled lemon (cut in half and add to fish, chicken, or vegetable stock)

1  3  4  6

**1.** Grate the aromatic yellow rind of the lemon without any of the bitter white pith underneath and reserve.

Measure out 1 cup (235 ml) of the Roasted Chicken Broth and refrigerate so that it is cold. In a large stock pot, bring the remaining stock to a boil.

**2.** In a large bowl, combine the cold broth, semolina, cheese, parsley, basil, nutmeg, and lemon zest.

**3.** Whisk until well blended.

**4.** Pour in the eggs (which we have broken into a measure first to make sure that no stray shell bits are included) and whisk to blend. Transfer the egg mixture to a container with a spout for easy pouring.

**5.** Stir the boiling broth in a circular motion to make a whirlpool in the center and begin pouring the egg mixture into the center.

**6.** Gradually drizzle the remaining egg mixture into the broth, stirring gently with a fork to form strands of egg shreds, and cook about 1 minute or until the egg has coagulated and the broth itself is clear.

**7.** Stir in the spinach and then season the soup to taste with salt and pepper and cook 1 to 2 minutes or until the spinach has wilted but is still bright green.

**8.** Taste for seasoning, and then divide the mixture among warmed soup bowls. Serve immediately, topped with more grated cheese if desired.

# Chapter 3

# FISH AND SEAFOOD SOUP/STEWS

Fish heads make the richest and tastiest broth.

IN MANY PARTS OF THE WORLD, people who live close to the sea have developed their own soups and stews. They range from light, brothy soups to rich, chunky stews, with no clear distinction between soups and stews. These soups are a challenge for those who rely on a retail market where fish are sold in fillet form and bones are not readily available. Try to patronize a fish market where the turnover is high.

Each region surrounding the Mediterranean makes its own version of fish soup. Saffron shows up in Spanish *zarzuela di mariscos* (seafood) and in French, bouillabaisse. Pastis, various anise-flavored spirits such as Pernod and Ricard, often flavor these soup/ stews. Rouille, a thick red pepper and garlic sauce enriches the Provençal Soupe de Poisson (page 52) in this chapter. Other entries in this category are orange-scented *bourride* from the French Languedoc and *suquet de peix* from Eastern coastal Spain, which typically contains saffron and almonds.

Italian versions include Neapolitan *zuppa de pesce* (literally, "fish soup"), *brodetto* from the province of Abruzzo, which always includes vinegar to cut the rich fattiness of Adriatic fish, and *burrida* from Liguria. The Cacciucco Livornese (page 47) in this chapter is a specialty of Livorno, and unique in that it is made with red, not white, wine. In San Francisco, *cioppino* is an adaption by Portuguese and Italian immigrants of traditional European fish stews.

In this chapter we also make Billi Bi (page 44), a most elegant soup made with the humblest of bivalves, mussels. The Caribbean Callalou Soup (page 50) is based on sweet crabmeat. The name refers to a various types of local cooking greens characteristic of island cooking.

The big choices here are whether to use shellfish and bivalves along with fish and whether the fish is whole or filleted. In more traditional fisherman's style, we use fish steaks on the bone to make the Cacciucco, but you may choose to make it with fillet. Many of the tastiest fish are also small and bony, so they are not suited to filleting but work very well in fish soup. Use a combination of fish with light, medium, and darker flesh for more complex flavor. Just be sure to warn your guests about small bones, which can be a choking hazard.

## SOUPMAKER'S TIP

**SOURCES FOR SEAFOOD BROTH:**
Open up a can of wild red salmon and clean away bones and skin. Save the juices and trimmings in a small freezer container and use it as a base for salmon chowder. Even the liquid contained in a can of tuna may be added in small quantities to fish soups. The same goes for the poaching liquid from cooking shrimp or other seafood or the juices given off by steaming mussels, clams, crabs, lobsters, or crayfish. Canned ocean clam broth has briny ocean flavor and is quite salty (so do not add salt to the broth), but it is a good choice for a quick seafood stock.

# BILLI BI

THIS CLASSIC SOUP is based on a traditional dish of the French province of Brittany on its western Atlantic coast, where mussels are abundant. There, the soup is known as *mouclade* and it is made with white wine, shallots, butter, egg yolks, garlic, a bouquet garni, *crème fraiche*, and either saffron or a dash of curry powder. One story is that Billi Bi was created by chef Louis Barthe in 1925 at Maxim's of Paris for one of his customers, William B. Leeks Jr., an American industrialist. The original Billi Bi didn't include any mussel meats but we like their soft, tender texture and mild flavor. Save a few mussel shells for garnish, if desired.

Ingredients for Billi Bi. This most elegant of soups is made from the inexpensive mussel.

**Makes about 3 quarts (3 L), serves 8 to 10**

### INGREDIENTS

- ½ teaspoon saffron threads
- 2 cups (475 ml) dry white wine, divided
- 2 pounds (907 g) mussels, well-scrubbed
- 3 to 4 sprigs fresh thyme
- ½ teaspoon crushed red pepper flakes
- 2 tablespoons (30 ml) olive oil
- 1 cup (100 g) thinly sliced celery
- 1 cup (160 g) finely diced onion
- 1 tablespoon (10 g) chopped garlic
- 2 tablespoons (16 g) all-purpose flour
- 1 cup (180 g) diced fresh tomatoes or canned chopped plum tomatoes
- ¼ cup (60 ml) brandy
- 2 tablespoons (30 ml) Pernod, Ricard or other unsweetened anise-flavored spirits
- 1 quart (1 L) Fish Stock, clam broth, or Vegetable Stock
- 4 egg yolks
- 2 cups (475 ml) heavy cream, divided
- Kosher salt and freshly ground black pepper

1

2   3

Soak the saffron in enough of the white wine to cover, 15 minutes, or until the liquid is bright yellow. Reserve. (See Appendix, page 149.)

**1.** Combine the remaining white wine, mussels, thyme, and red pepper flakes in a large soup pot. Cover and steam over high heat until all the mussels open, about 8 minutes, shaking the pot occasionally.

**2.** Strain the mussels into a colander placed over a bowl to catch the precious juices, known as the "liquor."

**3.** To ensure that no sand remains in the mussel liquor, pour it through a dampened paper towel or coffee filter laid inside a sieve (see Appendix, page 144) and reserve.

**4.** Meanwhile, in a second large stock pot (or wash out and reuse the first pot), heat the olive oil over medium heat. Add the celery, onion, and garlic, and sauté until fragrant, about 3 minutes.

**5.** Stir in the flour and cook for 2 to 3 minutes; add the tomatoes and continue cooking for a total of 5 minutes, or until the vegetables are crisp tender.

**6.** Pour in the saffron–white wine mixture, the brandy, and Pernod and cook for 3 to 4 minutes, until the flavors are combined.

Add the strained mussel juice and stock or clam broth to the pot. Bring to a boil and simmer together 5 minutes.

**7.** Meanwhile, remove most of the meat from the mussel shells, reserving the meat and discarding most of the shells. (You may wish to reserve some mussels in their shells, or just mussel shells, to use for garnish.)

**8.** To make the liaison (binder/thickener), whisk together the yolks and about ½ cup (120 ml) of the cream in a medium bowl. While whisking, pour in about 2 cups (475 ml) of the soup liquid to gently heat and temper the custard mix.

**9.** Pour the remaining cream into the pot and stir to combine.

**10.** Pour the custard mix into the pot. Heat while stirring until the soup thickens (165°F, or 74°C). Season to taste with salt and pepper. (If using the clam broth, salt will probably not be needed.)

**11.** Add the reserved mussels to the soup, stir to combine and serve immediately.

*(continued)*

# SOUPMAKER'S TIPS

✱ Farm-raised mussels sold in U.S. supermarkets—usually in 2-pound (907 g) bags—are already scrubbed clean. You will need to thoroughly scrub wild mussels, which are usually larger and more uneven in shape; pry off any barnacles before use as well. Do not pull the "beards" from the mussels until you are ready to cook them, as this keeps them alive. A live mussel's shell should close if it is tapped on a counter, so discard any mussels that do not close. In addition, discard any mussels that are closed, extra heavy, and make a dull sound when tapped; these may be "mudders," dead mussels filled with mud.

✱ The traditional rich egg yolk and cream liaison (binder) thickens the soup. Once this custard has been incorporated into the soup base, it is important not to boil it, but rather heat it only long enough for the yolks to thicken, 165°F (74°C). The same goes for reheating: If the soup gets too hot, the yolk mixture may curdle. If this does happen, you may strain out the mussel meats and blend the soup using a standard or immersion blender.

**SAVE FOR STOCK:**
Thyme stems, celery, onion, garlic, and tomato trimmings

# CACCIUCCO LIVORNESE

THIS COUSIN TO PROVENÇAL BOUILLABAISSE is a fisherman's stew from the Italian port city of Livorno and is traditionally made with five varieties of fish: one for every letter *c* in its name. Cacciucco was made with the assorted small fish known as *pesce povero* (poor fish) that the fisherman couldn't sell and brought home. The name comes from the Turkish *küçük*, meaning "small or bits," and perhaps originated on sixteenth century galleys, where it was prepared to feed the slaves. Here we use the fish heads to make a rich broth in which we poach the fish, which has been cut into steaks on the bone. This humble fish stew is traditionally made with whole fish left on the bone. If the potatoes are young with thin skins, leave them on, otherwise peel. This soup doesn't freeze well.

**Makes 1 gallon (4 L), serves about 8 as a main dish, 12 as a first course**

### INGREDIENTS

- 5 pounds (2.3 kg) assorted fish (see "Suggested Fish for Soup," Provençal Soupe de Poisson with Rouille, page 55)
- Bouquet Garni (recipe follows)
- 1 large onion, diced
- 1 small fennel bulb, finely chopped
- 2 teaspoons (6 g) chopped garlic
- ¼ cup (60 ml) extra-virgin olive oil
- 3 cups (540 g) chopped plum tomatoes (fresh, canned, or Tetra-Pak boxed)
- 1 cup (235 ml) red wine
- 1 pound (455 g) gold potatoes, halved and then sliced into ⅓-inch thick half-moons
- 2 tablespoons (5 g) chopped sage
- Sea salt and freshly ground black pepper
- Crostini (recipe follows)

**Fresh fish steaks cut from American red snapper, fluke, and porgy ready for the fisherman's pot**

Ask the fishmonger to gut, scale, and clean the fish and pull out and discard the bitter tasting gills. Have the fish cut into steaks (as shown) or fillets and the pin bones removed. Save the heads, "frames" (skeletons), and trimmings of white-fleshed fish only. Store the fish well chilled until ready to cook.

Rinse the fish heads and any other frames and trimmings in cold water.

**1.** Place the fish heads and any other trimmings along with the Bouquet Garni into a large soup pot, add 3 quarts (3 L) cold water, and bring to a boil.

**2.** Reduce heat to low and simmer, skimming as necessary, for 45 minutes or until the fish bones fall apart easily.

**3.** Strain the broth, pressing down well on the solids to extract all the juices. Reserve the strained broth. Clean out the pot and wipe dry.

**4.** In another pot, sauté the onion, fennel, and garlic in olive oil.

**5.** Add the tomatoes and red wine.

**6.** Pour the strained fish broth into the pot and bring back to a boil.

**7.** Add the potatoes and boil over moderate heat until the potatoes are almost tender, about 8 minutes.

**8.** Stir in the sage and season to taste with salt and pepper.

**9.** Just before serving, add the fish according to size (larger, firmer fish first, then smaller, softer fish), and simmer until the fish flakes, about 10 minutes.

**10.** Serve the cacciucco in large bowls accompanied by Crostini (recipe follows) and garnished with a sage sprig if desired.

### BOUQUET GARNI:

- 2 large sprigs Italian parsley
- 2 large sprigs fresh thyme
- 2 large strips orange zest, cut using a potato peeler
- 1 whole, dried small dried red chile
- 2 bay leaves

Make a bouquet garni (see Appendix, page 149) by tying together the parsley, thyme, orange zest, chile, and bay leaves in kitchen string or in a piece of muslin tied shut.

### CROSTINI:

- 3 to 4 cloves garlic
- ½ cup (120 ml) extra-virgin olive oil
- 12 to 16 slices firm, crusty Italian bread

# SOUPMAKER'S TIPS

❊ Typical bony strong-flavored fish from the Tyrrhenian Sea, the portion of the Mediterranean off the coast of Livorno, for Cacciucco, would include the dragon-faced *scorfano nero* (black scorpionfish) and *gallinella* (Tub Gurnard) all flavored with tomato, garlic, chili, red—never white—wine, and fresh sage. If desired, have the fishmonger fillet the fish and pull out the pin bones and use the heads, bones, and any trimmings to make the broth, substitute the filets for the fish steaks.

### SAVE FOR STOCK:

Onion, fennel, and tomato trimmings; parsley and thyme stems; remaining strips of orange zest (use to flavor spiced fruit or chutney; freeze if desired to use at a later date); the fruit of the orange (cut away the white flesh remaining and cut the fruit into slices, half-moons, or cubes and add to salad)

1 2

Preheat the oven to 375° F (190°C, or gas mark 5).

**1.** Crush or finely mince the garlic, using a garlic press if desired, and mix with the olive oil.

**2.** Cut the bread on the diagonal into ½-inch (1 cm) thick slices. Arrange in a single layer on a baking tray. Brush the garlic-oil mixture onto both sides of the bread slices. Bake 15 minutes or until golden brown.

# CARIBBEAN CALLALOU SOUP

A DELICIOUS CELEBRATION SOUP made in different versions throughout the Caribbean islands, Callalou gets its name from the greens used in it, such as taro, amaranth, or other island-specific greens. However, a mild tasting cooking green such as spinach, Swiss chard, or Chinese spinach make a good substitute. The soup also contains coconut milk and crabmeat, which are typical of Caribbean cooking. Another ingredient, okra (of African origin), can often be found at farmers' markets. Fresh, young okra is pleasingly chewy and quite delicious. Frozen sliced okra can be substituted but tends to be slippery and should be added during the last minutes of cooking. For those who don't want to eat pork, substitute diced smoked turkey leg or thigh for the bacon and cook the vegetables in vegetable oil.

**Makes about 1 gallon (4 L), serves 8 to 12**

**INGREDIENTS**

- ½ pound (225 g) bacon, cut into small bits
- 1 medium onion, diced
- 1 red bell pepper, diced
- 2 ribs celery, diced
- 1 pound (455 g) okra, ends trimmed off, sliced ½-inch thick
- 1 tablespoon (10 g) chopped garlic
- ¼ cup (32 g) all-purpose flour
- 2 quarts (2 L) Vegetable Stock or Chicken Stock (page 14 or 3)
- 1 tablespoon (15 ml) Jamaican Pickapeppa sauce, or substitute Worcestershire sauce
- 2 cans (14 ounce, or 397 g) unsweetened coconut milk
- 2 tablespoons (4.8 g) chopped fresh thyme, or 2 teaspoons (5.5 g) dried thyme
- 2 bay leaves
- 1 pound (455 g) best-quality crabmeat, picked over for shells
- ¼ pound (115 g) baby spinach
- Kosher salt and freshly ground black pepper
- 2 tablespoons (30 ml) hot pepper sauce (optional)

In a large soup pot, cook the bacon until crispy and brown, pouring off excess fat (you'll need ¼ cup, or 60 ml).

Add the onion and cook in the bacon mixture until softened but not brown, about 5 minutes.

1. Add the pepper, celery, okra, and garlic.

2. Stir well to combine.

3. Add the flour and cook the mixture about 5 minutes, stirring, to remove the raw flour taste.

4. Add the stock and Pickapeppa or Worcestershire.

5. Add the coconut milk, thyme, and bay leaves and simmer 15 minutes.

6. Just before serving, stir in the crabmeat.

7. Add the spinach leaves and heat through until spinach is wilted, about 2 minutes.

8. Season with salt and pepper to taste and add hot pepper sauce, if using. Serve piping hot.

## SOUPMAKER'S TIPS

❉ Bacon is easiest to work with if it is semifrozen. You may cut presliced bacon into thin strips and then cut the strips into small squares. Alternatively, you can cut the bacon into chunks and then process them to small bits, but this will work only if the bacon is firm and semifrozen. The same technique works for pancetta.

**SAVE FOR STOCK:**
Onion trimmings, red bell pepper cores and stems, celery leafy tops and tougher bottoms, garlic skins, thyme stems.

# PROVENÇAL SOUPE DE POISSON WITH ROUILLE

THIS CREAMY SOUP is made from the fisherman's catch of various small, local fish along the French Mediterranean coast and is served with *croûtes* (toasted slices of French bread) spread with rouille, a garlic-laden red pepper sauce. Here we use four fish: black sea bass, fluke (also known as summer flounder), porgy (a cousin of Mediterranean sea bream), and collagen-rich cod. Use about 1 pound (455 g) of fish for 1 quart (1 L) water along with shellfish trimmings such as scallop "catch" muscles shrimp shells, lobster bodies (gills removed and discarded), and/or the steaming liquid from clams, mussels, or crab—the more variety, the better the flavor. Ask your fishmonger to prepare the fish by removing the gills from the head, scraping out the blood line from either side of the backbone, and cutting the fish into steaks. This soup is best if made in larger quantities, as using a variety of fish gives it the best flavor; it freezes well.

**Makes about 5 quarts (5 L), serves 12 or more**

### INGREDIENTS

- 1 cup (235 ml) extra-virgin olive oil, divided
- 1 large onion, diced
- 1 leek, diced (see Appendix, page 153)
- 1 small fennel, chopped (use the bulb and lighter colored stalks)
- 6 cloves garlic, crushed
- 2 pounds (907 g) red ripe tomatoes, cored and roughly chopped
- 5 pounds (2.3 kg) whole fresh fish, cut into steaks, including the heads
- Bouquet garni (see Appendix, page 149)
- ¼ cup (60 ml) Pernod, Ricard, or other unsweetened anise-flavored spirits, or 1 tablespoon (6 g) crushed fennel seed
- 1 gallon (4 L) cold water
- ½ teaspoon saffron threads
- 1 cup (235 ml) white wine
- 1 baguette, sliced on the diagonal ½-inch (1 cm) thick, toasted
- Sea salt and freshly ground black pepper
- ¼ pound (115 g) crushed spaghetti or cappellini
- 2 cups (475 ml) Rouille (recipe follows)
- ½ cup (30 g) chopped Italian parsley

1. Heat ¾ cup (175 ml) of the olive oil in a large soup pot. Cook the onion, leek, fennel, and garlic until softened but not browned, about 5 minutes, and then add the tomatoes.

2. Wash the fish steaks in cold water and drain.

3. Add the fish and other ingredients up through the Pernod to the pot.

4. Pour in the cold water and bring to a boil over medium heat (if the heat is too high, the fish may stick to the bottom and burn).

5. Simmer 30 to 40 minutes, skimming as necessary, or until the fish bodies fall to pieces. While soup is simmering, soak the saffron threads in the white wine (see Appendix, page 149).

6. Blend, bones and all, using an immersion blender, if available, to extract the maximum flavor and body from the soup. This step is optional but recommended.

7. Using, ideally, a food mill, strain the blended soup mixture. (The last juices to be squeezed out will be the tastiest.) Alternatively, strain through a sieve, pressing down firmly on the solids with a special cone-shaped wooden pusher or the back of a ladle.

8. Rinse the soup pot and then return the strained liquid to the pot. Add the saffron-wine mixture, season with sea salt and black pepper to taste, and bring to a boil.

When ready to serve, add the crushed spaghetti to the pot and boil about 8 minutes or until almost tender with a small hard white core in the center.

9. Place one or two rounds of toasted bread in the bottom of large soup bowls and top with about 1 tablespoon (15 ml) of the Rouille.

10. Ladle the soup and spaghetti over top, sprinkle with parsley. Serve the soup piping hot.

# ROUILLE

Rouille ("roo-ee") is a thick dip or sauce made from soft bread, red peppers, garlic, saffron, chili peppers, and generous quantities of fruity olive oil. A specialty of Provençal cuisine, it is served as a flavorful enrichment for fish and fish soup. It makes a wonderful sandwich spread or topping for grilled or roasted vegetables.

**Makes about 3 cups (705 ml), about 24 servings**

### INGREDIENTS

- 2 large thick slices hearty French or Italian bread, crusts removed and diced (about 2 ounces, or 55 g, by weight)
- ¼ cup (60 ml) fresh lemon juice (one average lemon yields about 3 tablespoons, or 45 ml, of juice)
- Pinch saffron threads (optional)
- 1 large or 2 smaller roasted and peeled red bell pepper, homemade or purchased
- 1 roasted hot red chile pepper (or substitute hot ground red chile powder such as cayenne, Turkish marash pepper, or hot paprika)
- 2 cloves peeled garlic
- 4 ounces (115 g) blanched almonds, chopped
- ¼ cup (15 g) Italian parsley leaves
- 1 teaspoon (6 g) kosher or sea salt
- ½ cup (120 ml) extra-virgin olive oil

Ingredients for Rouille including kosher salt, French bread, roasted red peppers, garlic cloves, thyme, hot red pepper flakes, and extra virgin olive oil.

**1.** Cut off and discard the crust of the bread. Soak the bread in water to cover until soft, about 5 minutes. Squeeze out the liquid.

**2.** Place the bread, lemon juice, saffron (if using), red pepper, chile pepper, garlic, almonds, parsley, and salt into the bowl of a food processor and process until smooth.

**3.** With the motor running, slowly pour in the olive oil to make a thick, creamy sauce with the texture of mayonnaise. Store covered and refrigerated up to 2 weeks. The sauce should be thick enough to hold its shape. If it is too thick—more like peanut butter than mayonnaise—thin with roasted pepper juice or water.

Store Rouille covered and refrigerated up to 2 weeks.

# SOUPMAKER'S TIPS

❋ Ask the fishmonger for fish "frames," the skeletons left after removing the fillets. You may be able to get them at no or low cost. Ask the fishmonger to remove the bitter tasting gills. Fish heads are best here as they are full of flavor and will add rich body to the soup. All fish and fish trimmings should have a sweet, briny smell, never a "fishy" smell, a sign of a less than fresh fish.

❋ To make Soupe de Poisson ahead, cool and then freeze the strained soup broth and add the spaghetti later.

❋ If the cooked fish bones are relatively small, discard them in the garbage disposal. Larger bones should be discarded in the trash. Double-bag the discards to keep them from smelling up the kitchen.

**SAVE FOR STOCK:**

Onion skins, tops, and tails; leek rootlets and lighter green leaves; fennel outer leaves and light colored stalk portions; garlic skins; tomato cores; and parsley, basil, and thyme stems

## SUGGESTED FISH FOR SOUP

| | |
|---|---|
| Arctic Char | Usually farm raised from Canada |
| Barramundi | Australian fish now farm raised in the United States |
| Branzino (Mediterranean Sea Bass) | Mostly farm raised but relatively expensive |
| Cod | Light flavor, full of natural gelatin, which gives the soup good body |
| Croaker and other Drumfish such as Red Drum | Bony but flavorful and inexpensive |
| Flatfish, such as fluke, flounder, sole, halibut, sand dab, Dover sole, and European turbot | High in gelatin with lean white flesh |
| Grouper | From Florida, the Caribbean, and the Gulf of Mexico |
| Haddock | Similar to cod, also quite gelatinous |
| Halibut | From the Atlantic and the Northern Pacific |
| Monkfish | Once a lower-priced fish, now in high demand so the price has gone up |
| Pollock | Often found frozen, from Alaska; mild flavor |
| Red Mullet | Excellent flavor, not often found in the United States, though goatfish is similar |
| Red Snapper, Yellowtail Snapper | Makes a delicate soup with pleasing flavor; usually high in price |
| Rockfish | All sorts of smaller rockfish can work well for soup |
| Sea Bass | Delicate, pleasing flavor; found on the Atlantic Coast |
| Sea Bream (dorade) | Usually farm raised from the Mediterranean or Porgy; the Atlantic equivalent |
| Striped Bass (Hybrid Striped Bass) | Has less flavor than wild striped bass but acceptable |
| Weakfish | Bony sea trout; light flavor; good, less expensive choice for soup |
| Whiting | Good choice as this bony but lean fish is usually inexpensive |

Stronger-tasting darker-meat fish such as bluefish, mackerel, tuna, mahi-mahi, or salmon can be used but in small quantity so as not to overpower the flavor of more delicate fish.

# Chapter 4
# POTAGES, PURÉES, AND CREAMY BISQUES

This vegan Senegalese Peanut and Yam Soup has a fragrance of cinnamon and clove.

FIRST CAME POTTAGE, a thick soup or stew made from vegetables, grains, and sometimes meat or fish boiled for several hours until the mixture was quite soft and well-cooked. The long cook time ensured that the food was safe for consumption and easy to eat by people who often lacked teeth. Pottage was a food of serfs and peasants in Great Britain from Neolithic times and a staple of the poor throughout most of Europe from medieval to late Renaissance times. The pot would be kept on the fire for days with more ingredients added as soup was ladled out. Pottage was served with bread for sopping. The French potage, a country-style simple vegetable-based soup, shares the same root.

Purées are cooked food, usually vegetables or legumes that have been ground, pressed, blended, or sieved to a consistency somewhere between a thick liquid like heavy cream and a soft creamy paste like mashed potatoes. The word is of French origin and originally meant purified or refined. The Italian Chestnut Soup with Fennel and Marsala (page 64) is a purée thickened with sweet, nutty chestnuts and flavored with licoricelike fennel and nutty-tasting fortified Marsala wine. The Senegalese Peanut and Yam Soup with Ginger (page 60), a vegan soup, is a purée of yams and peanuts fragrant with sweet spices.

Bisque descended from pottage and was originally made from game meat and birds, especially pigeon and quail. In the classic French kitchen, bisque was a thick rich strained purée usually made from the pulverized and strained shells of crustaceans—at first crayfish, but also lobster and shrimp—as is the classic French Lobster Bisque with Cognac (page 69) in this chapter.

In the mid-seventeenth century, the French word *bisque* was imported into English and was originally spelled *bisk*. Though the origins of the word are murky, some tie it to the Spanish Atlantic province of Biscay, or *Vizcaya* in Spanish. Others believe it came from biscuit (*bis cuit* means "twice cooked") because the crustaceans are first sautéed in their shells and then simmered in aromatic broth. Rich and creamy seafood bisque is traditionally served in a low two-handled cup on a saucer or in a mug.

Lobster bisque may have developed as a way to use culls, lobsters that have only a single claw, or a tiny second claw, and are therefore worth less money at the market. Another early name for bisque was a *coulis*, or *cullis* in English, which was a puréed and strained soup. Today, coulis usually refers to a strained fresh fruit or tomato sauce. The Tomato Bisque with Basil and Fennel (page 62) shares smooth texture, pink color, and velvety rice thickening with classic shellfish bisques.

In this chapter, we also make a vegan fresh Corn Cream Soup with Summer Vegetables (page 58) that gets its creaminess from ground and strained sweet corn. The Hungarian Woodlands Mushroom Soup (page 66) is a hearty mushroom lover's soup infused by dried and reconstituted porcini mushrooms gathered in the wild through Western and Eastern Europe and dried for use throughout the winter.

# CORN CREAM SOUP WITH SUMMER VEGETABLES

THIS VEGAN SOUP is as delicious as fresh corn munched off the cob and well worth the task of preparing the corn. The blended corn makes a sweet, creamy broth without any dairy products; the diced summer vegetables add color and crunch; and the generous sprinkling of fresh herbs makes for a fragrant soup. A similar soup is made in Japan: *oumorokoshi no kurímusúpu* (Corn Cream Soup), which is often garnished with sliced, fried lotus blossoms for crunch.

**Makes about 1 gallon (4 L), serves 8 to 12**

### INGREDIENTS

- 8 ears young sweet corn
- 2 quarts (2 L) Corncob Stock (page 10), or Vegetable Stock (page 14)
- 1 jalapeño, seeded and cut up
- 2 bay leaves
- 4 cups, about 1½ pounds (680 g), diced firm vegetables in small pieces: summer squash, zucchini, yellow and red bell peppers, tender green beans, carrots, or shelled baby limas or edamame (the last two can be used frozen but should be rinsed of any frost)
- 2 large beefsteak tomatoes, cored and diced
- Kosher salt and freshly ground black pepper
- About 3 cups (90 g) picked tender herb leaves (including ½ cup (15 g) mixed chopped tender herbs: tarragon, thyme, chives, parsley, basil, mint, and/or marjoram), chopped (see Appendix, page 147 amd 148)

# SOUPMAKER'S TIPS

If your zucchini and yellow squash are large, cut away the seedy core and save for stock. Dice the outer meaty portion of the squash and add to the soup. Large yellow crookneck squash especially will contain a tough, woody seed section that is best removed.

**SAVE FOR STOCK:**

Tops and ends of summer squash and zucchini; seedy cores and stems of yellow and red bell peppers; tomato trimmings; corncobs; and tender herb stems but not mint, which is too strong for most stocks.

Prepare the corn cream by cutting the kernels off the cobs. See Appendix, page 145.

**1.** Combine the corn kernels, corn "milk" stock, jalapeno, and bay leaves in a large soup pot. Bring to a boil, reduce the heat, and simmer for 20 minutes, stirring occasionally, or until the mixture has thickened.

**2.** Skim off and discard the white foam that rises to the top.

Purée the soup in a blender until smooth and velvety in texture. Transfer the liquid back into a large soup pot and bring to a boil.

**3.** Add diced vegetables and bring back to a boil. Simmer 10 minutes or until crisp tender.

**4.** Add the diced tomatoes and bring back to a boil.

**5.** Stir to combine and then season to taste with salt and pepper.

**6.** If desired, transfer the soup to a tureen.

**7.** Sprinkle with the chopped herbs and stir to combine.

**8.** Serve the soup immediately.

Store refrigerated up to 4 days. This soup does not freeze well.

# SENEGALESE PEANUT AND YAM SOUP WITH GINGER

PEANUT SOUP appears on the menu in many West African countries. In the early 1500s Europeans brought peanuts from South America to Africa, where they caught on quickly because of their similarity to the native African bambarra groundnut. Yams were first domesticated in Central America or South America about 5,000 years ago. This smooth, creamy soup made with vegetable stock and thickened with both peanuts and peanut butter gets its sweetness from yams. A warm reddish brown, the vegan soup is fragrant with sweet, earthy, and piquant spices. Many African Americans serve this soup to celebrate the seven days of Kwanzaa. The soup freezes perfectly. You may substitute Chicken Stock if desired.

Ingredients for vegan Senegalese Peanut and Yam Soup with Ginger—showing Northern white sweetpotatoes and Southern red yams

**Makes about 1 gallon (4 L), serves 8 to 12**

### INGREDIENTS

- 2 tablespoons (30 ml) canola or other vegetable oil
- 1 large onion, chopped
- 1 tablespoon (10 g) chopped garlic
- 2 tablespoons (12 g) chopped ginger root
- 2 teaspoons (5 g) ground cumin
- 2 teaspoons (4 g) ground coriander
- 1 teaspoon (2 g) ground cinnamon
- ½ teaspoon (1 g) cayenne pepper or other ground hot chile pepper
- Pinch ground cloves
- 2 cups (360 g) diced fresh ripe tomatoes or canned chopped plum tomatoes
- 2 pounds (907 g, or about 2 large) yams, peeled and cut into large chunks
- 2½ quarts (2.5 L) Vegetable Stock, (page 14) simmering
- 1 cup (145 g) roasted peanuts
- ½ bunch cilantro, leaves and tender stems chopped, plus extra for garnish
- ½ cup (130 g) peanut butter (chunky or smooth) Salt and fresh ground black pepper

1. Heat the oil in a large Dutch oven or soup pot over medium heat. Sauté the onion until lightly browned, about 6 minutes. Stir in the garlic, ginger, cumin, coriander, cinnamon, cayenne, and cloves. Sauté 2 to 3 minutes to release the fragrance. Stir in the tomatoes and yams and continue to cook, stirring occasionally, about 5 minutes.

2. Add the hot stock. Add the peanuts, bring to a boil, reduce heat, and simmer 30 minutes or until the yams are quite soft. Remove the soup from the heat.

3. Strain the soup through a sieve or wire basket, as shown here, reserving the solids and liquid separately.

Place the solids into a blender, adding enough liquid to cover by 1 inch (2.5 cm). Start the blender on low, gradually increasing the speed. Do not fill the blender jar more than two-thirds full. Purée the soup until smooth.

4. Return the soup to the pot. Whisk in the peanut butter and chopped cilantro, season to taste with salt and pepper, and heat through.

5. Top each serving with the chopped cilantro. Serve piping hot. Garnish with more chopped peanuts and diced tomato, if desired.

# SOUPMAKER'S TIPS

Be sure to wash the cilantro thoroughly, as field-grown cilantro is often quite sandy. If you see a lot of sand in the bowl of cilantro after you wash it, wash again in another bowlful of cold water.

**SAVE FOR STOCK:**
Onion trimmings, garlic skins and ends, tomato and yam trimmings, ginger trimmings (good for chicken stock)

**SORTING OUT THE CONFUSION:**
Yams, sweet potatoes, and sweetpotatoes: Sweet potatoes originated in the New World and traveled to the Old World well before the potato. The English word *yam* derives from the Senegalese *nyami*, a starchy African root with rough brown skin that can grow to 5 feet (1.5 m) in length and 150 pounds (68 kg) in weight. Botanists now prefer to use *sweetpotato* (one word) instead of *sweet potato* (two words) to distinguish this member of the Morning Glory family. In the 1930s Louisiana growers chose the name *yam* to set their vivid orange, soft-fleshed, sweet storage roots apart from the drier, paler white-to-gold-fleshed sweetpotato traditionally grown in the North. The boniato, a staple from Mexico to Vietnam, is a starchy white-skinned sweetpotato with yellow flesh, dry, fluffy texture, and delicately sweet chestnutlike flavor. The Okinawa, a Hawaiian sweetpotato called *poni* in Hawaii, turns lilac after cooking and has rich, sweet flesh. Asian sweetpotatoes are rose-skinned, ivory-fleshed cultivars, which fall between the drier boniatos and moist-flesh whites in taste and texture.

# TOMATO BISQUE WITH BASIL AND FENNEL

SUMMERTIME IS HEAVEN for tomato lovers and this soup makes use of the best juicy, ripe tomatoes from the garden or the farmers' market. A far cry from canned cream of tomato soup, this bisque gets its velvety texture from white rice and its scent from sweet basil and licorice-like fennel. You'll be disappointed if you make this soup from tasteless, mealy, out-of-season tomatoes. But in season, it's a great way to use up less-than perfect ultra-ripe tomatoes that may have bad spots that need to be trimmed away. The riper the tomato, the better the soup.

**Makes about 1 gallon (4 L), serves 8 to 12**

### INGREDIENTS

- 4 tablespoons (59 ml) extra-virgin olive oil, divided
- 1 large white onion, cut into chunks
- 3 cloves garlic
- 3 pounds (1.4 kg) ripe beefsteak-type red tomatoes, cored and cut up into large chunks
- ½ cup (97.5 g) white rice, uncooked (not instant)
- 3 sprigs basil on the branch
- 6 cups (1.4 L) Vegetable Stock (page 14)
- 1 head fennel, cut into small dice
- 1 pound (455 g) ripe beefsteak-type red and/or yellow tomatoes, cored and diced (see Appendix, page 150)
- ¼ cup (10 g) basil chiffonade (see Appendix, page 150)
- 1 cup (235 ml) heavy cream
- Kosher salt, cayenne pepper, and freshly ground black pepper

A celebration of summer tomatoes with fragrant sweet basil. Low-acid yellow tomatoes are sometimes available at farmers' markets and supermarkets.

In a large soup pot, heat 2 table-spoons (30 ml) of the olive oil, add the onion and garlic, and cook until softened but not browned, about 5 minutes.

**1.** Add the 3 pounds (1.4 kg) cut-up beefsteak tomatoes and stir to combine with the onions and garlic.

**2.** Pour in the rice and basil sprigs.

**3.** Add the Vegetable Stock. When pouring in this and any other stock, leave behind the last ½ inch (1 cm) or so of liquid because the solids settle to the bottom. Bring to a boil, reduce heat, and simmer until the rice is creamy and quite soft, stirring occasionally, about 20 minutes.

**4.** Transfer the mixture to a blender jar, filling the container only about halfway and working in two to three batches.

**5.** To prevent splattering of the hot liquid, start blending on low speed and hold on to the lid to keep it from popping off. Then increase speed and blend to a smooth purée.

**6.** Strain the purée, discarding any remaining solid bits, seeds, and skin, and reserving the strained purée.

**7.** Wash out the pot and add the fennel and remaining 2 tablespoons (30 ml) of olive oil. Sauté the fennel until tender but not browned about 10 minutes, stirring often.

**8.** Add diced tomatoes and basil chiffonade and cook until the tomatoes are softened but still hold their shape. Add the reserved strained tomato purée and bring to a boil.

**9.** Pour in the heavy cream, bring to a boil, and season with salt, cayenne, and black pepper.

**10.** Serve immediately garnished with basil chiffonade or a basil sprig.

Store soup refrigerated for up to 4 days or freeze if desired.

**SAVE FOR STOCK:**
Onion, tomato, fennel trimmings and basel stems.

# ITALIAN CHESTNUT SOUP WITH FENNEL AND MARSALA

THIS FRAGRANT, RICH, DEEP-FLAVORED soup has a base of the salt-and-pepper cured pork belly called *pancetta* in Italian. Bacon makes the best substitute, though if it is fatty, some of the fat should be discarded. Sweetly nutty Marsala wine (the dry type is best here) from the island of Sicily adds flavor and a slight kick. Dry sherry, Madeira, or even Tuscan Vin Santo, a dessert wine made from raisin-grapes, will also work. Chestnuts and fennel is a natural pair; both are in season in autumn and in high demand in Italy, where most of the world's chestnuts are grown. The sweet, starchy-nutty chestnuts are lightened and accented by the fennel bulb and its more intensely anise-flavored seeds. Prepared chestnuts are available frozen and vacuum sealed in bags or glass jars. The stalks of the fennel bulb are also used here; they have a much stronger anise flavor than the bulb.

**Makes 3 quarts (3 L), serves 12**

### INGREDIENTS

- 2 tablespoons (28 g) unsalted butter
- ¼ pound (115 g) pancetta, cut into small bits
- 1 large onion, chopped
- 1 fennel bulb, trimmed and chopped including the stalks
- 2 tablespoons (12 g) ground fennel seed
- 2 bay leaves
- ¼ teaspoon ground cloves
- 2 quarts (2 L) Chicken Stock (page 9)
- 1½ pounds (680 g) peeled cooked chestnuts
- ½ cup (120 ml) dry Marsala
- ½ cup (120 ml) heavy cream
- Kosher salt and freshly ground black pepper
- Thinly sliced chives and/or finely chopped fennel fronds, for garnish

**1.** In a large soup pot, melt the butter, add the pancetta, and then cook over low to moderate heat until the fat has rendered out, stirring constantly.

**2.** Add the onion, fennel, ground fennel seed, bay leaves, and cloves, and cook, covered, for about 15 minutes, or until the vegetables have softened.

**3.** Add the Chicken Stock and chestnuts and bring back to a boil.

**4.** Simmer 45 minutes, skimming as necessary, or until the chestnuts are soft enough to break apart easily.

**5.** Blend the soup using an immersion blender as shown here, or transfer the soup, working in several batches, to the jar of a blender and blend.

**6.** Strain through a sieve or a food mill to achieve a smooth, velvety consistency.

**7.** Transfer soup to a clean pot and add the Marsala and the cream. Bring back to a boil, and season to taste with salt and pepper.

**8.** Pour the soup into individual serving bowls and garnish with chives. Serve the soup immediately.

**SAVE FOR STOCK:**
Onion and fennel trimmings, any extra pancetta fat (excellent cooked with beans)

# HUNGARIAN WOODLANDS MUSHROOM SOUP: GOMBALEVES

THIS IS A VEGETARIAN SOUP for mushroom lovers! Its base, cremini mushrooms, also known as baby bellas or brown mushrooms, are the same variety as the common white button mushroom but with darker skin and a closed cap, earthy flavor, and dense, meaty texture.

We combine these hearty cultivated mushrooms with reconstituted dried wild woodland porcini (*Boletus edulis*). Hungarian paprika (dried powdered sweet paprika peppers) and sour cream are characteristic Hungarian flavorings. This soup freezes very well.

**Makes about 1 gallon (4 L), Serves 8 to 12**

### INGREDIENTS

- 1 large onion, chopped
- 1 tablespoon (10 g) chopped garlic
- 6 tablespoons (85 g) unsalted butter
- 2 pounds (907 g) cremini mushrooms, diced (see "Slicing and Dicing Cremini Mushrooms," page 68)
- 1 ounce (28 g; about 1 cup) dried porcini mushrooms, reconstituted and chopped (see "Using Dried Porcini Mushrooms," page 68)
- 2 tablespoons (14 g) sweet Hungarian paprika
- 6 tablespoons (47 g) all-purpose flour
- 3 quarts (3 L) Mushroom Stock (page 13), simmering, divided
- ½ cup (30 g) chopped Italian parsley
- Kosher salt and freshly ground black pepper
- 1 cup (230 g) sour cream (optional), for garnish

1. In a large, heavy soup pot, sauté the onions and garlic in the butter until the onions are softened but not browned.

2. Add the chopped cremini and chopped porcini.

3. Cook until the mushrooms give off their liquid and the liquid evaporates, about 10 minutes.

4. Stir in the paprika.

5. Add the flour, stir to combine and cook together about 5 minutes to get rid of the raw flour taste.

6. Pour in about half the stock, here Mushroom Stock made from cremini and shiitake stems and porcini mushroom liquor. Bring to a boil while stirring, until thick and smooth.

7. Pour in the remaining stock, bring back to a boil, stir in the parsley, and season with salt and pepper to taste.

8. Ladle soup into individual serving bowls—here we serve it in mini-French "lion's head" bowls as part of a tasting menu or hors d'oeuvres party. Top each portion with a dollop of sour cream and serve.

**SAVE FOR STOCK:**
Onion trimmings, garlic peels and ends, extra cremini stems, extra porcini liquor

# TECHNIQUES

## Using Dried Porcini Mushrooms

Known as *cêpes* in France, *steinpilz* or "stone mushroom" in Germany, and *porcino* (singular), which means "piglet," in Italy (pigs are fond of eating them), this prized "king of mushrooms" forms a symbiotic association with living trees in deciduous and coniferous forests. The best porcini (plural) will include large slices of light-colored mushroom caps. Dark, broken porcini may be full of dirt, so soak well, and then strain the soaking liquid carefully. Instead of gills, long, thin tubes fill the undersides of the caps of members of the *Bolete* family.

**1.** Place the porcini in a bowl and add water to cover; use boiling water if you're pressed for time, cold water if not. Soak the porcini to until they are plump and soft, about 20 minutes in boiling water or about 1 hour in cold water.

**2.** Use a slotted spoon to scoop the porcini from their soaking liquid, which should be deep brown in color after soaking. Place the reconstituted porcini in a bowl and reserve.

**3.** Strain most of the porcini liquor through a dampened paper towel placed in a sieve over a bowl or other container. Reserve the delicious juices, or freeze it for later use.

**4.** Leave behind and discard the last portion of soaking liquid, which will often contain a lot of dirt.

**5.** Chop the mushrooms into small bits.

## Slicing and Dicing Cremini Mushrooms

Use this same technique to slice and/or dice common white button mushrooms or other firm, fresh mushrooms. If the mushrooms are little tired and soft, you must slice them one at a time in order to cut through the tougher skin.

If the mushrooms have long stems, cut them away flush with the bottom of the cap or pull off the stems and reserve for Mushroom Stock, freezing if desired.

2

**1.** Line up the mushroom caps with the stem side down. Push the mushrooms one at a time toward the knife while taking care to keep your fingers away from the edge. Slice by pivoting from the point of the knife and cutting downward.

**2.** Lay the sliced mushrooms down flat on a work surface and cut into rough bits, working from one side of the pile to the other. Once you've cut the mushrooms into rough bits, begin chopping the mushrooms, continuing until they are chopped into small bits 1/4 to 1/2-inch (6 mm to 1 cm) across.

# LOBSTER BISQUE WITH COGNAC

IN FRENCH CUISINE, a bisque is a velvety-smooth, creamy, highly seasoned soup that is classically made from crustaceans, especially lobster and crayfish, but also crab and shrimp. By extension, other smooth, creamy soups, especially if thickened with white rice, may also be termed *bisque* (see Tomato Bisque with Basil and Fennel, page 62). In making this lobster bisque, you'll be extracting every bit of flavor from the lobsters including their shells and their delicious roe, if you can find mature female lobsters. Although this is a rather complex soup to make—that is, preparing live lobsters and then chopping or grinding their shells, which contain a surprising amount of flavor—the results are superb and fit for the most elegant of dinners. The bisque also freezes surprisingly well.

**Makes about 3 quarts (3 L), serves 12**

### INGREDIENTS

- 2 live lobsters (or crayfish) (1½ pounds, or 680 g, each), preferably female for their beautiful and delicious roe
- 2 tablespoons (30 ml) olive oil
- 6 tablespoons (89 ml) Cognac
- ½ cup (120 ml) Madeira or dry sherry
- 2 carrots, peeled and sliced
- 2 ribs celery, trimmed and sliced
- 1 medium onion, cut into rough chunks
- 2 ripe red tomatoes, quartered
- 4 cloves garlic, halved
- Bouquet garni (see Appendix, page 149): 3 sprigs tarragon, 2 sprigs thyme, 1 sprig flat-leaf parsley, and 1 bay leaf
- 2 tablespoons (32 g) tomato paste
- 3 quarts (3 L) Shrimp or Chicken Stock (page 9)
- 3 tablespoons (42 g) unsalted butter, softened
- ¼ cup (31 g) all-purpose flour
- 1 cup (235 ml) white wine
- 2 cups (475 ml) heavy cream
- Salt, white pepper, and cayenne pepper
- Thinly sliced chives and/or cooked lobster roe (see Appendix, page 151), for garnish

1. Place one live lobster on a work surface with its head facing your non-dominant hand.

2. Grip the lobster on the back of its thorax, or main body shell (the lobster's claws will have been secured by rubber bands). Look for the place where two sections of shell meet. Plunge the point of a sharp chef's knife between the shell sections. This will kill the lobster instantly although it will often keep moving.

3. Split one of the lobsters lengthwise from head to tail. Separate the two halves. Remove and discard the two halves of the "sand sac" (the small bag) from inside both sides of the head, which is the lobster's stomach, and the long fingerlike spongy gills from underneath the main body portion. Repeat the process for the second lobster.

4. Remove the dark green roe sacs and reserve. (The more mature the female lobster, the darker and more abundant the roe will be.) Cook the roe, crumble it, and reserve (see Appendix, page 151).

5. Cut or twist off the claws from both lobsters. Break up the claw shells by hitting with a meat pounder or a hammer.

6. Cut off and reserve the lobster tail sections (two halves from each lobster). Separately, cook the tail pieces in oil until the meat is opaque and the shells curl up. Cool and reserve.

7. In a large sauté pan or rondeau (as shown here), heat the olive oil till it's just beginning to smoke. Cook all the lobster pieces except the reserved tail sections, at high heat till they turn bright red. Add the Cognac and Madeira and flambé, taking care to keep your face averted when lighting.

8. Add the carrot, celery, onion, tomatoes, garlic, and bouquet garni to the pot. Cook together 5 minutes.

If using a skillet, scrape the lobster-vegetable mix to a large heavy-bottomed soup pot. Add tomato paste and Chicken Stock and bring to a boil. (If using a rondeau, add the liquid directly to the contents of the pot.) Simmer 1 hour, stirring occasionally to prevent sticking.

Strain out solids, reserving both solids and broth separately and reserve pot—it is not necessary to wash it. Chop the solids into smaller pieces using a heavy chef's knife or cleaver. The smaller the pieces, the more flavor you'll be able to extract from the shells.

9. Mix the lobster pieces and broth together in a large soup pot.

**10.** Make a beurre manié (a soft paste of the butter and flour).

**11.** If available, add the lobster roe to the paste, reserving some for garnish, if desired.

**12.** Mash the roe together with the butter and flour to make a creamy paste.

**13.** Whisk the beurre manié into the broth to thicken it. Add the white wine and bring back to a boil. Then, reduce heat and simmer 1 hour or until the lobster shells have given off their flavor, skimming as necessary and stirring occasionally.

Skim off any foamy impurities that rise to the surface and discard.

**14.** Meanwhile, cut the cooked tail meat into thin crosswise slices and reserve for garnish.

**15.** Strain the mixture first through a colander, sieve, or china cap, pressing down firmly with the back of a ladle to extract all the good flavors. Discard the solids. Strain a second time through a fine sieve or china cap for smooth texture and to make sure no shell pieces remain.

**16.** Transfer the strained liquid to a large pot. To finish the bisque, stir in the cream, bring back to a boil, and season with salt, white pepper, and cayenne to taste. It should be fluid and creamy, thick enough to lightly coat the back of a wooden spoon.

**17.** Ladle bisque into hot soup plates and sprinkle with reserved sliced lobster meat, chives, and any reserved cooked roe. Serve immediately.

Store refrigerated up to 3 days. This soup may be frozen.

**SAVE FOR STOCK:**
Carrot, celery, onion and tomato trimmings, garlic skins, herb stems

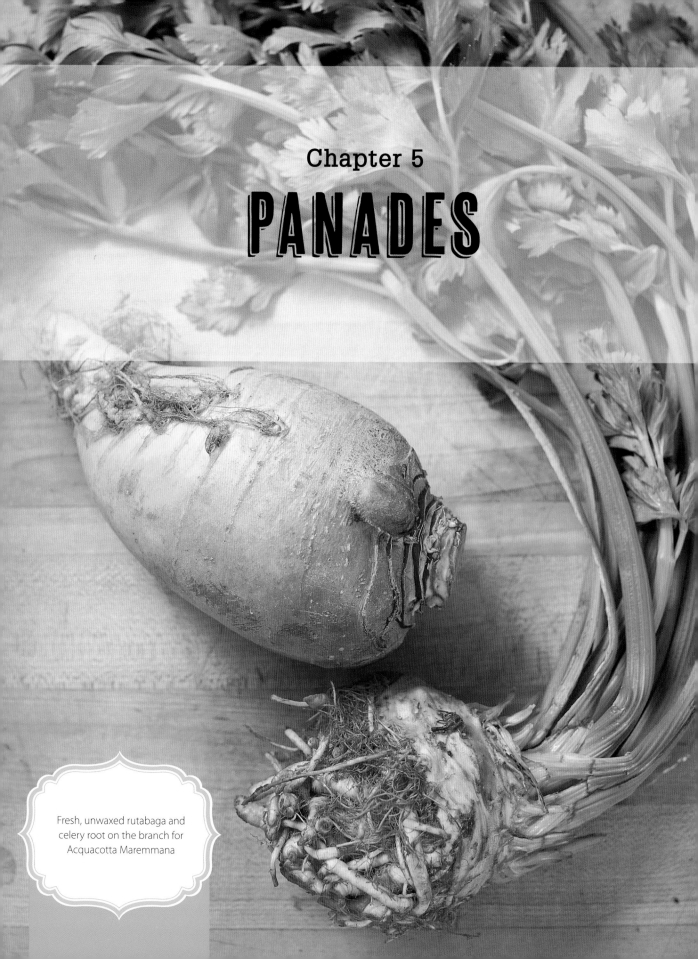

# Chapter 5
# PANADES

Fresh, unwaxed rutabaga and celery root on the branch for Acquacotta Maremmana

ONE OF THE OLDEST FORMS OF SOUP, panades are soups based on leftover stale bread, often toasted, which thickens the soup by absorbing its liquid. *Panade* comes from the Latin word for bread (*panis*). The related word, *pap*, as in the Pappa al Pomodoro in this chapter, comes from a Latin word for children's food similar to porridge. Bread-based soups were a common peasant food because stale bread, often baked in large loaves in the village oven once a week, was too precious to throw away and could be used as a way to stretch small amounts of assorted vegetables, cheeses, meats, or other ingredients to make a soup that was filling enough to be served as a main dish, sometimes with an egg poached in the broth as in the Acquacotta Maremmana in this chapter.

The broth could be made from meats, poultry, vegetables, or seafood in the case of bouillabaisse, cacciucco, and related seafood soups. More simply, the liquid could be water (as in Acquacotta), wine in France and southern Europe, beer in northern Europe, or raw vegetable juices (as in Golden Tomato Gazpacho with Smoked Paprika, page 138). Milk could also be used, often in a sweet cinnamon-scented soup—a more liquid form of bread pudding.

Bread soup is mentioned in a tenth-century Arab cookbook, *Kitâb-al-tabîj*. An old Arab bread soup, known as *tarid*, was made from crumbled bread, garlic, coriander, and water, a possible forbear of gazpacho. In Provence, *soupe á l 'ail* (garlic soup), rich with eggs, exotic peppercorns, and generous amounts of olive oil all poured over toasted bread slices, was presented by a new wife to her husband in the hope that their lives would be equally rich and abundant.

*Açorda*, a Portuguese bread soup, legacy of centuries of Arab presence in the Iberian Peninsula, is most common in the south of the country where the Arab influence is strongest. Inland, açorda is made from pork meat and sausages, but on the seacoast, açorda is made from fish and shellfish.

Cacciucco alla Livornese, Spanish zarzuela, and many others (see chapter 3, "Fish and Seafood Soup/Stews") are one-dish fish soups or stews made with whatever small bony fish and random shellfish the fishman or fishmonger had leftover at the end of the day and are served over toasted bread rubbed with garlic to sop up the juices. In Germany and Scandinavia, rye breads are used to make *schwarzbrotsuppe* (black bread soup) and Danish *ollebrod* (beer bread soup), which dates back to medieval times and still popular today as a morning-after hangover remedy. It is made from stale pumpernickel bread and dark beer simmered with honey, cinnamon, and lemon.

One must for bread soup is crusty bread, which will keep its shape when soaked in liquid; soft bread will just dissolve into a sticky paste. In Italy, ciabatta, focaccia, and other substantial, chewy breads are sliced, toasted, and placed in the bottom of the bowl with the soup ladled over top. Other bread soups are thickened with crumbled bread simmered until it breaks down (see Pappa al Pomodoro, page 81, and Green Gazpacho with Garlic, Grapes, and Almonds, page 140).

# ZUPPA PAVESE

THIS QUICK AND NOURISHING peasant soup originated, according to legend, in 1525 when King Francis I of France was defeated by King Charles V of Spain at the Battle of Pavia. The king took refuge in a nearby farmhouse where the woman of the house was preparing soup. To make her humble soup fit for a king, she fried stale bread, placed it in a bowl, added two poached eggs, and ladled broth over top and finished it with a sprinkling of Grana Padano (the hard, grating cheese of the region). The soup pleased the king who asked for the recipe to be given to his servant. It is actually a traditional peasant soup long prepared in the region of Pavia in Lombardy with ingredients at hand, such as the Grana Padano cheese and either chicken, beef, or veal broth.

**Makes about 3½ quarts (3.5 L), serves 6**

### INGREDIENTS

- 6 thick slices (4 ounces, or 115 g) crusty, substantial French or Italian bread
- ¼ cup (60 ml) extra virgin olive oil, or 4 tablespoons (70 g) unsalted butter, softened
- ¼ pound (115 g) freshly grated Grana Padano cheese, divided
- 2 tablespoons (30 ml) white or cider vinegar
- 6 eggs
- 2 tablespoons (8 g) finely chopped Italian parsley
- 3 quarts (3 L) Beef Stock (page 8) or Roasted Chicken Broth (page 20)
- Sea salt and freshly ground white pepper

Preheat the oven to 350°F (180°C, or gas mark 4). Warm six large oven-proof soup bowls.

Brush the bread slices with olive oil or spread with butter. Arrange on a baking sheet and bake until golden brown, about 10 minutes.

**1.** Place a slice of bread in the bottom of each bowl and sprinkle each with 1 tablespoon (5 g) of cheese.

Meanwhile, bring a medium wide-mouthed pot of salted water to a rolling, vigorous boil. Add the vinegar, which helps to firm the eggs when poached. Crack one egg at a time into a small bowl or other container. This ensures that no shell pieces are added to the broth.

**2.** Pour the egg into the water. Repeat until you've added all the eggs to the boiling vinegared water.

Cook the eggs about 2 minutes or until the whites have set on the outside but the yolks are still quite liquid.

**3.** Use a slotted spoon to scoop the poached eggs from the water and transfer one at a time to the pre-pared bowls. Discard any raggedy edges from the eggs before adding to individual soup bowls. Sprinkle with parsley.

Meanwhile, in a medium pot, bring the Beef Stock or Roasted Chicken Broth to a boil. Season to taste with salt and pepper.

**4.** Sprinkle cheese on each egg.

**5.** Pour or ladle the boiling broth over the eggs. Serve with more cheese to sprinkle on at the table.

**6.** The egg should still be soft in the center and enriches the broth when broken.

**SAVE FOR STOCK:**
This is such a thrifty soup that no trimmings will be left for stock other than a few parsley stems.

# FRENCH ONION SOUP

WHEN THE GREAT open Paris wholesale market of Les Halles was still open (it was demolished in 1971), hungry truckers and late-night revelers alike would head there in the early hours of the morning to get their bowl of burn-your-tongue-hot reviving onion soup topped with a croûte (toasted slice of French bread) under a blanket of broiled Gruyère cheese. One of the world's best known soups today,

French onion soup became a perennial on U.S. restaurant menus during the heyday of French cooking in America in the 1960s. Because few restaurants, especially chains, prepare their own rich, hearty beef stock, relying on additive-laden concentrated commercial beef base instead, your homemade soup will likely be far superior to any you've had in any but the best restaurants.

**Makes about 1 gallon (4 L), serves 8 to 12**

### INGREDIENTS

- ¼ pound (1 stick, or 115 g) unsalted butter
- 5 pounds (2.3 kg) (about 6 large) Spanish onions, sliced
- 2 tablespoons (26 g) sugar
- 2 bay leaves
- 3 sprigs fresh thyme, tied with kitchen string (see Appendix, page 153)
- ¼ cup (1 ounce, or 31 g) all-purpose flour
- 1 cup (235 ml) dry red wine
- 1 gallon (4 L) Beef Stock (page 8)
- Kosher salt and freshly ground black pepper
- 3 tablespoons (45 ml) brandy
- 1 crusty baguette, sliced (stale bread preferred) and toasted until firm and brown
- ½ pound (225 g) Gruyère or Emmenthal cheese, grated or sliced

1
4
6  8

## SOUPMAKER'S TIPS

If desired, for extra flavor, brush the bread slices with olive oil or beef drippings (the fat from a roast of beef) and then rub with a cut clove of garlic before toasting.

**SAVE FOR STOCK:**
Onion trimmings (outer layers of skin, tops, and tails)

9

Melt the butter in a large pot with a wide bottom over medium heat.

**1.** Add the onions and stir to mix with the butter.

**2.** Stir in the sugar, which helps the onions brown.

**3.** Add the bay leaves and thyme; here we made a bouquet garni, tied it with kitchen string, and then tied it to the handle of the pot to make it easy to fish out.

**4.** Cook until the onions are very soft and evenly caramelized to a deep brown color, about 30 minutes, stirring often preferably with a wooden spoon or silicone spatula to avoid scraping up any metal bits into the soup.

**5.** Sprinkle the flour over the onions and stir to combine. Reduce the heat to medium low so the flour doesn't burn, and cook for 10 minutes to get rid of the raw flour taste.

**6.** Add the wine and stir to deglaze the browned bits from the bottom of the pot.

**7.** Add the Beef Stock and 1 quart (1 L) of water, bring the soup back to a simmer, and cook for 10 minutes, or until the broth is smooth and slightly thick, stirring occasionally. Discard the bay leaves and thyme sprigs. Season to taste with salt and freshly ground black pepper and, just before serving, stir in the brandy.

**8.** When you're ready to serve, preheat the broiler. Ladle soup into French-style lion-head soup bowls,

or other heat-proof soup bowls. Top each portion with one to two toasted baguette slices.

**9.** Sprinkle generously with cheese, making sure to cover the toasts completely.

Arrange bowls on a metal tray and then place under the broiler for about 3 minutes, or until the cheese has browned and is bubbling. Or, arrange the toasted baguette slices on a baking sheet in a single layer, sprinkle with the Gruyère and broil until the cheese is bubbly and golden brown, 3 to 5 minutes. Top each serving of soup with one or two cheese croûtes.

**10.** Serve the soup, which will be piping hot, so take care not to burn your mouth.

# FRENCH SOUPE DE POTIRON
## (Red Pumpkin Soup)

THIS PANADE SOUP thickened with toasted sourdough bread makes a striking presentation if made from and baked and served right in a French "Cinderella pumpkin." Known in French as *rouge vif d'etamps*, this giant, flattened, brilliant red pumpkin may be found in farmers' markets in autumn and is the perfect size and shape for this traditional French dish. If not available, make the soup with a sugar pumpkin, also known as a pie pumpkin with its crooked neck and rough skin. Jack-o-lantern pumpkins are too stringy. An alternative is to make it from a speckled green and orange Spanish calabaza, commonly found in Latino markets or use a squat Korean ridged tan pumpkin. Vegetable stock may be substituted for the customary chicken stock, and the soup can be served for a vegetarian Thanksgiving meal. The soup does not freeze well.

**Makes about 1½ gallons (6 L), serves about 12**

**INGREDIENTS**

- 6 ounces (167 g, or 1½ sticks) unsalted butter
- 1 pound (455 g) sourdough bread, thickly sliced
- 1 pound (455 g) leeks, trimmed of dark green portions, sliced and washed thoroughly (see Appendix, page 153)
- 1 tablespoon (2.5 g) chopped fresh sage leaves
- 1 teaspoon (3 g) freshly grated nutmeg
- Salt and freshly ground black pepper
- 1 large cooking pumpkin weighing about 10 pounds (4.5 kg)
- 2 tablespoons (30 ml) vegetable oil
- ½ pound (225 g) gruyere or sharp cheddar cheese, shredded
- 6 cups (1.5 L) Chicken Stock (page 9) or Roasted Chicken Broth (page 20), simmering
- 1 cup crème fraiche, for garnish
- Sprigs of sage, for garnish

Preheat the oven to 350°F (180°C, or gas mark 4).

**Two squat French red pumpkins ready to stuff and bake for a bread-thickened (panade) soup**

1. In a large skillet, melt the butter and allow it to brown for nutty flavor, but do not allow the butter to burn.

2. Arrange the bread slices in a single layer on a baking tray. Brush both sides with about half the browned butter, reserving the remainder. Bake 12 to 15 minutes or until golden brown. Reserve, leaving the oven on.

3. Add the leeks to the skillet containing the remaining brown butter. Cook the leeks over moderate heat, stirring often, until they are soft and tender, about 10 minutes.

4. Remove from the heat, season leeks with sage, fresh grated nutmeg as shown, salt and pepper, and reserve.

5. Place the pumpkin on a sturdy baking tray. Use a marker to draw dotted lines in a rough circle measuring about 6 inches (15 cm) from the center of the pumpkin.

6. Using the marker, join the dots together to draw a circle.

7. Using a serrated knife and working in an up and down sawing motion, create a lid by cutting through the ink circle.

8. Pull off the lid and reserve.

9. Use a large sturdy metal spoon to scoop out any seeds and strings from the pumpkin and from the bottom of the lid.

10. Rub the outside of the cleaned lid and ready-to-stuff pumpkin with the oil. Season the inside of the pumpkin with salt and pepper.

11. Make a layer of half the toasted bread inside the pumpkin.

12. Top with half the leeks.

12  13  14  15

16  17

**13.** Sprinkle with half the cheese. Repeat layering the bread, leeks, and cheese.

**14.** Pour in the stock so that the pumpkin is about two-thirds full—the pumpkin itself will give off a lot of liquid as it cooks. Fit the lid onto the pumpkin.

**15.** Bake until the pumpkin begins to soften and brown on the outside and the stock bubbles on the inside, about 1½ hours. Pierce the side of the pumpkin near the top edge. The pumpkin should be tender but still firm enough to hold its shape. Bake 15 minutes longer if necessary.

**16.** Carefully remove the baking dish from the oven, remove the lid and set aside. Using a long-handled metal spoon, gently scrape the softened flesh away from the sides of the pumpkin and into the soup, taking care not to pierce the skin.

**17.** Serve the soup including a portion of the pumpkin flesh in large bowls, top each portion with a dollop of crème fraiche, and garnish with a sprig of sage.

## SOUPMAKER'S TIPS

❊ Place the pumpkin on a paella pan, a deep-dish pizza pan, a large ceramic quiche pan, or a large cast iron skillet for baking.

❊ If the pumpkin does collapse, use a baster to sop up the excess liquid from the pan and transfer to a pot or a large measure. Bring the liquid to a boil. Serve the soup in bowls and pour a portion of the hot liquid over top.

**SAVE FOR STOCK:**
Bread ends (use to thicken soup or to make bread-crumbs), leek trimmings, inner pumpkin scrapings, pumpkin seeds (dry, salt, and roast for a delicious, healthy snack)

# PAPPA AL POMODORO

THIS THRIFTY TUSCAN home cook's soup depends on the juiciest, ripest fresh tomatoes, preferably tasty heirloom varieties, and the best fruity green extra virgin olive oil. It is even better made a day ahead and reheated or it may be served cool—not ice cold, which would deaden its delicate flavor. Like other dishes of *la cucina povera* (Italy's cuisine of the poor), pappa al pomodoro has become a fashionable restaurant dish. In summertime, some cooks layer sliced bread, olive oil, chopped garlic, chopped basil, diced tomato, and salt and pepper, and soak it in water or broth for a cold summer soup-salad that is a second cousin to Golden Tomato Gazpacho with Smoked Paprika (page 138). The soup is vegan (and vegetarian) if made with vegetable stock.

**Makes about 1 gallon (4 L), serves 8 to 12**

### INGREDIENTS

- 2 medium onions, finely diced
- 4 garlic cloves, minced
- 6 tablespoons (89 ml) extra-virgin olive oil
- 4 pounds (1.8 kg) ripe beefsteak tomatoes, cored and coarsely chopped and/or canned ripe tomatoes
- 4 to 6 sprigs fresh basil, tied in a bundle with kitchen string
- 3 quarts (3 L) Vegetable or Chicken Stock (page 14 or 9)
- 1 loaf (1½ pounds, or 680 g) stale hearty Italian bread, crusts removed and diced
- Salt (preferably sea salt) and freshly ground black pepper
- Basil chiffonade (see Appendix, page 150) and extra-virgin olive oil, for garnish

**1.** In a large soup pot, sauté the onion and garlic in the olive oil until softened but not browned, 3 to 5 minutes. Add the chopped fresh tomatoes, if using, and the basil sprigs, bring to a boil, and cook over medium heat until softened, about 15 minutes.

**2.** Add the Stock and canned tomatoes (if using) and bring to a boil.

**3.** Reduce heat and simmer until the soup is thick, about 20 minutes. Remove and discard the basil sprigs.

**4.** Add the bread cubes and stir to combine. Simmer 20 minutes longer or until the bread is quite soft. Season soup generously with salt and pepper.

**5.** Pour soup into individual serving bowls, sprinkle in the fresh basil Chiffonade and drizzle generously with best quality extra-virgin olive oil just before serving.

**SAVE FOR STOCK:**
Onion, garlic, and tomato trimmings, basil stems, save extra bread to make croutons or cut into small bits and process in the food processor to make homemade breadcrumbs.

# ACQUACOTTA MAREMMANA

ACQUACOTTA, OR "COOKED WATER," a specialty of the Tuscan Maremma, was prepared and eaten in the field as a one-pot meal by the region's shepherds and horseback cattlemen. Greens such as chard and Tuscan kale are essential. Seasonal vegetables such as zucca (hard pumpkin-like squash), garden peas, zucchini and yellow crookneck squash, fennel bulb, broccoli Romanesco, chard stems, and green beans are cut into bite-size pieces and mixed with shelled fresh cranberry, borlotti beans, and/or fava beans. In Italy's weekly town and city markets, each produce vendor sells his or her own mixture of cut-up vegetables, so it's easy to make this nourishing vegetarian soup. Each portion includes a poached egg. Some cooks prefer to beat the eggs with grated pecorino (sheep's milk) cheese and pour it into the soup while stirring to make raggedy shreds.

**Makes about 1 gallon (4 L), serves 8 to 12**

### INGREDIENTS

- 1 cup (235 ml) extra-virgin olive oil, divided
- 2 ribs celery, trimmed and sliced
- 2 carrots, trimmed and diced
- 2 medium onions, trimmed and diced
- 1 small head fennel, trimmed and diced
- 1 small whole hot dried red chile pepper
- About 2 pounds (900 g) diced mixed firm seasonal vegetables, such as zucchini, yellow squash, butternut squash, eggplant, green beans, celery root, turnip, parsnip, and rutabagas—the more kinds, the better the soup
- 1 bunch chard greens or Tuscan kale, stems removed, washed and cut into thin strips, and/or ¼ savoy cabbage, cored, shredded, and cut into short lengths (see "Cutting Cabbage into Shreds," page 85)
- Stems from 1 bunch chard, thinly sliced (preferably ruby chard)
- 1 pound (455 g) ripe round tomatoes, diced (don't bother skinning unless you're using thick-skinned plum tomatoes)
- 3 quarts (3 L) boiling water
- Sea salt and freshly ground black pepper, optional
- 1 loaf crusty Italian bread, sliced about ¾-inch (1.5 cm) thick on the bias
- 8 to 12 large extra-fresh eggs, preferably thicker-shelled brown-shell eggs
- ¼ pound (115 g) grated pecorino cheese, preferably milder Pecorino Toscano

1

4    5

1. Place half the olive oil and the celery, carrots, onions, fennel, and hot pepper in a large heavy-bottomed soup pot. Cook together until crisp tender, about 5 minutes; then, add the mixed vegetables. Bring back to boil and cook 5 minutes or until crisp tender.

2. Add the greens and ruby-chard stems and stir to combine. Bring back to a boil and cook over medium heat until the greens are soft, stirring once or twice.

3. Add the tomatoes and cook together until the vegetables are mostly tender, about 20 minutes.

4. Add the boiling water and simmer 15 minutes longer or until the vegetables are quite tender, adding more water as needed to make a chunky soup with a moderate amount of broth and skimming as needed. Add salt and pepper to taste, if desired.

Meanwhile, toast the bread slices until golden. Drizzle with the remaining olive oil.

5. Just before serving, crack open the eggs one at a time into the boiling soup. Allow the eggs to poach in the soup until the whites are set but the yolks are still liquid, 3 to 4 minutes, ladling boiling soup over top to cook the whites evenly.

6. To serve soup, place one or two slices of toasted bread in the bottom of individual large soup bowls. Using a slotted spoon, scoop out the poached eggs and place one on top of the bread in each bowl (don't worry about white shreds of eggs, which will remain in the soup).

## SOUPMAKER'S TIPS

If serving only a part of the soup, poach only enough eggs to serve one per portion as the eggs should be poached with a liquid center, not hard cooked.

**SAVE FOR STOCK:**
Celery trimmings, carrot tops and tails, onion trimmings, chard stems, tomato cores, zucchini tops, yellow squash tops, eggplant trimmings, fennel (tough outer layers, trimmings, larger stalks), green beans ends, and celery root parings.

7. Ladle the soup broth and vegetables over the eggs and then sprinkle each portion with cheese and serve.

# TECHNIQUE

## Cutting Cabbage into Shreds

Here we use a mild, curly-leaf Savoy cabbage, preferred in Italy where it is known as *verza*. Choose a head with bright, crisp, dark green outer leaves. As the cabbage ages, produce workers will pull off the outer leaves—a head with only lighter green leaves on the outside has been on the shelves too long.

**1.** Place the cabbage on the work surface holding it steady with your nondominant hand. Using a sharp chef's knife, cut the cabbage in half.

**2.** Lay one half of the cabbage with its flat side down and the root end away from your body. Slice in half again.

**3.** Place one cabbage quarter on the work surface with a flat side down and the root end toward your body. Slice away the core, angling the cut down away from the root end.

**4.** Use the tip of your knife to cut away any remaining core section. Discard the core, which is too strong-tasting for stock, unless you're making cabbage soup.

**5.** Lay the cored quarter down and cut into 1-inch (2.5 cm) slices, keeping the slices together.

**6.** Turn the sliced quarter 90 degrees and cut into thin shreds, about ⅓-inch (1 cm) thick.

**7.** Repeat until you've cored, sliced, and shredded all the cabbage quarters.

# Chapter 6
# BEAN SOUPS

Mirepoix is the foundation of many soups, especially those of French and Italian traditions.

WHETHER IT'S A VEGAN CECI E TRIA, (page 89), chickpea soup redolent of garlic and rosemary, or a Charleston Black Bean Purée with Madeira and Lemon (page 93), here is a whole world of hearty bean soups to explore. The chunky vegetarian Greek Lentil Soup (page 96) is even better made with firm, nutty French green lentils. The classic Turkish Red Lentil Soup (page 98) is fast cooking because it is made with skinned and split red lentils. This Italian *Pasta e Fagioli*, meaning "pasta and beans," (page 101) may be a soup, a stew, or a dish of pasta.

Mirepoix (diced onion, carrot, celery, and, in this case, garlic) cooked in butter or olive oil is the aromatic foundation of many soups, especially those from French and Italian traditions. Celeriac, or celery root, is often combined or substituted for branch (or Pascal) celery, and leek may be included for a sweeter onion flavor. Depending on the recipe, parsnips, garlic, tomatoes, shallots, mushrooms, and bell peppers may form part of the mirepoix. Elsewhere, chiles and ginger flavor the soup foundation. In the Creole and Cajun cooking of Louisiana, onion, green pepper, and celery, along with thyme, form "the holy trinity" essential to gumbo and other typical soups and stews. Garlic, parsley, or shallots may be included.

Italian *soffritto* is a mixture of finely diced onion, garlic, celery, and sometimes garlic, shallots, and herbs slow cooked in olive oil. Portuguese *refogado* (onions, garlic, and tomato), Spanish *sofrito* (chopped onion, garlic, and tomato), and Catalan *sofregit* (tomatoes, onions, olive oil, garlic, and onions, and sometimes mushrooms and peppers) are all slow cooked in olive oil. In Germany and other Northern European cuisines, *suppengrün* (soup greens) are sold in bundles and usually include leek, carrot, celeriac, and perhaps parsnip. In the case of Ashkenazi Jewish cooking, the soup greens will include dill and Hamburg parsley root.

## Soupmaker's Note

Legumes contain high percentages of iron and fiber, little to no fat of their own (except for soybeans and peanuts), and no cholesterol. They are high in both soluble and insoluble fiber, provide almost as much calcium as milk, and have significant amounts of potassium, zinc, and magnesium. Combine them with grains or a small amount of animal protein, and you've got a complete protein. Lentils, chickpeas, and soybeans are highest in protein.

# SOUPMAKER'S TIPS

**COOKING BEANS:**

✳ **Buy top quality beans:** Quality and freshness matter. Look for harvest-dated beans and choose the freshest. The fresher the beans, the easier and quicker they will be to cook, the less likely they will be to break apart, and the easier they'll be to digest. Canned beans work better as an addition to a vegetable soup, not a soup entirely based on beans, because the taste of the can and the bland quality of canned beans would dominate it.

✳ **The beginner bean:** If you're new to bean eating, start with skinned, split legumes such as yellow or green split peas, split red lentils, split dried fava beans, or Indian white urud dal. The skins are the most difficult part of the bean to digest. Red kidney beans have the thickest skin; white cannellini beans and black turtle beans have thin, tender skins.

✳ **Use soft water:** In hard water, especially chickpeas, beans may stay hard even after hours of soaking and cooking. Add about ⅛ teaspoon of baking soda per pound of dried beans to hard water to neutralize the acid. Don't overdo the baking soda, as it can cause the skins to separate, and cause the beans to get mushy and leach out their nutrients into the water.

✳ **Get the dirt out:** Many older bean recipes start with the admonition to pick through and rinse the beans. In most cases this isn't necessary today. However, black turtle beans and certain imported legumes may contain small lumps of debris, so pick over and rinse them to be on the safe side.

✳ **Prevent fermentation:** Beans are prone to fermenting. If you make a pot of bean soup in hot weather, place it in a sink half-filled with ice water to chill quickly. Once cold, bean soup can be refrigerated in an airtight container for up to four days, or they can be frozen.

✳ **Blanch beans for easing digestibility:** In the most tradition-bound areas of the Mediterranean, beans are blanched or par-cooked. They are placed in a large pot, preferably earthenware, brought to a boil and cooked for five minutes, then drained and rinsed under cold water. This extra step is not necessary but is a good idea when cooking beans that may be several years old or if your system is not accustomed to them.

✳ **Add hardening ingredients last:** Wait until the beans are at least halfway cooked before adding salt, sugar, and acid (such as vinegar, tomato, or molasses), which harden the skin of the beans and prevent them from softening.

✳ **Add salt to the soaking water for beans**, which will help them maintain their shape when cooked. Leave out the salt if you want the beans to break apart and help to thicken the soup.

# CECI E TRIA
## (Pugliese Chickpea and Semolina Noodle Soup)

THIS SOUP COMES FROM the Italian province of Puglia, which is at the heel of the "boot" and surrounded by water. The region's ancient name, Messapia, means "land between two waters"—the Ionic Sea and the Adriatic Sea. The soup is a fine example of *la cucina povera*, meaning "cuisine of the poor." Those in poverty, by necessity, would transform the simplest of local ingredients—here we use chickpeas simmered with garlic and rosemary—to make a delicious and satisfying dish. A combination of chewy boiled homemade semolina noodles with crunchy fried noodles adds textural excitement to the palate.

**Makes about 1 gallon (4 L), serves 8 to 12**

### INGREDIENTS

- ¾ pound (340 g) dried chickpeas, soaked overnight in cold water to cover, with a pinch of salt
- 8 to 10 cloves garlic, sliced
- 2 bay leaves
- 3 to 4 sprigs rosemary
- ¼ cup (60 ml) extra-virgin olive oil
- Sea salt and freshly ground black pepper
- 1¼ pounds (567 g) Tria Pasta (recipe follows), divided
- 1½ cups (355 ml) olive oil or extra-virgin olive oil, for frying
- 1½ cups (355 ml) vegetable oil, for frying

1. Drain and rinse the chickpeas. Place chickpeas in a heavy-bottomed soup pot and add 1 gallon (4 L) cold water. Bring to a boil, skimming off the abundant white foam.

2. Add the sliced garlic, bay leaves, rosemary, and olive oil and simmer until the chickpeas are half-tender. Add the salt and pepper to taste.

3. Continue cooking until the chickpeas are quite tender but still whole. Remove and discard the bay leaves and rosemary sprigs.

Have ready a wire cooling rack placed on top of a baking tray or paper towels or brown paper for draining the fried noodles.

4. Heat the oils for frying together in a medium heavy-bottomed pot to 365°F (185°C). Sprinkle about one-third of the tria noodles into the pot. Although it is counterintuitive, keeping your hand close to the oil when adding the noodles is safer as it helps prevent splattering when the noodles hit the oil. Stir the noodles with a metal or wooden spoon so they fry evenly (see page 92).

5. Allow the noodles to fry until golden brown, about 5 minutes.

6. Use a wire skimmer, known as a "spider," or a slotted spoon to remove the noodles from the oil.

7. Place on a wire rack to drain. Because the rack allows for air circulation above and below, the noodles will stay crisp.

When the soup is almost ready, bring a large pot of salted water to a boil and cook the remaining tria pasta until almost, but not quite, tender and chewy, about 8 minutes.

8. Scoop from the water and add to the soup just before serving.

9. Top each portion with a handful of the crunchy fried tria and serve immediately.

# TRIA PASTA

Here we make a simple dough of finely milled semolina and water, without eggs as is done in Puglia, where 80 percent of Italy's semolina is raised. Semolina, the glassy inner endosperm of durum wheat, is hard, grainy, and golden yellow with a mellow, nutty flavor. It is milled in various grades of fineness; the finer, the better for pasta. The finest semolina is known as "remacinata" because it is ground twice. Unlike the protein in bread flour, the protein in durum semolina is highly extensible, meaning that it can be rolled out without snapping back like a rubber band.

**Makes about 1¼ pounds (567 g)**

- 10 ounces (284 g) fine semolina
- 7 ounces (207 ml) warm water

**1.** Make a well with the semolina and add the water. Use a fork to mix the semolina into the water.

**2.** Mix and knead well until the dough is soft and elastic.

**3.** Wrap in plastic wrap or cover with a damp towel and allow the dough to rest and hydrate at room temperature for about 1 hour. The dough will soften considerably as it rests.

**4.** Pat the dough with more semolina. Roll out dough to the thickness of a sheet of cardboard (about ¼ inch, or 6 mm) with a rolling pin. Do not roll out thinly.

**5.** Using a knife (here a straight-bladed Italian pasta knife) or a wheeled pasta cutter, cut the dough into 2- to 3-inch (5 to 7.5 cm) wide ribbons. Sprinkle the ribbons with more semolina to keep them from sticking to each other.

**6.** Cut each strip into ½-inch (1 cm) wide strips.

**7.** Or, stack three or four ribbons that have been well dusted with more semolina on top of each other. Cut into ½-inch (1 cm) wide strips. If the dough is too soft or the ribbons haven't been dusted with semolina, the strips will stick together.

**8.** Rub the cut strips lightly in your hands to separate them and then toss with semolina.

**9.** The strips are now ready to cook immediately or to spread out and leave to dry on a semolina-dusted tray or a mesh pasta drying rack for up to 3 hours. (The pasta is best cooked while still soft.)

# SOUPMAKER'S TIPS

✳ All beans, but especially chickpeas, give off a large quantity of white foam at the beginning of cooking, which consists of the protein impurities contained in the beans (chickpeas are among the legumes highest in protein). Skimming off the foam will help make a lighter, clearer soup that is easier to digest.

✳ If your chickpeas are old and very dry and/or if the water in your area is very hard (high in minerals and acidic), add just a pinch of baking soda to neutralize the acidity and soften the chickpeas. Don't be tempted to add more, because it will turn the chickpeas to mush and reduce their nutritional value.

✳ To save the frying oil for use another time, set up a large sieve inside a clean, dry larger bowl—you want to make sure it contains no water bubbles which would make the oil splatter when heated. Line the inside of the sieve with a paper towel or large coffee filter. While the oil is still hot (the oil is much thinner when hot), carefully pour the oil through the filter into the bowl. Allow the oil to cool to room temperature and then transfer into a clean, dry container. Reuse the oil next time you deep-fry, adding about 20 percent new oil each time you use it and discarding after one or two more uses or when the oil darkens.

**SAVE FOR STOCK:**

Here is one soup where there is little to save for stock. However, any excess chickpea cooking liquid makes a full-bodied stock for other soups. In fact, that liquid will actually jell when it gets cold due to the pectin it contains.

# TECHNIQUE

## Checking the Temperature of Frying Oil without Using a Thermometer

Although using a frying thermometer will give the most accurate results, here are two ways of checking the temperature without any special tools.

**1.** Hold your hand about 3 inches (7.5 cm) above the oil. If the air feels quite hot, the oil is ready. You can also see that the oil in the pot is forming wavy lines across the bottom, which happens as the oil temperature goes up.

**2.** Or, stick the end of a wooden spoon into the oil. If lively bubbles form around the handle, the oil is hot enough.

# CHARLESTON BLACK BEAN PURÉE WITH MADEIRA AND LEMON

BLACK BEANS have a notably fine grain when cooked, and when simmered with ham hocks, puréed, and strained, the resulting soup has a smooth, velvety texture that is easy to digest because the bean skins have been removed. This soup dates back to a nineteenth-century marketing campaign to make black beans more acceptable to white Americans who were scared off by their deep purple (not actually black) color and strong association with foods eaten by slaves. Renamed "turtle beans," they were promoted as a way to make a low-cost mock turtle soup, an upper-class delicacy traditionally laced with Madeira, which is a fortified wine made on the Portuguese island of Madeira and imported into Charleston from precolonial times. The chopped egg mimosa garnish—named for its resemblance to yellow mimosa tree blossoms—the ground mace, and the lemon zest echo the traditional flavorings for turtle soup.

**Makes about 1 gallon (4 L), serves 8 to 12**

### INGREDIENTS

- 4 smoked ham hocks, about 3 pounds (1.4 kg)
- 2 gallons (8 L) Chicken or Vegetable Stock (page 9 or 14)
- 2 pounds (4 cups, or 907 g) dried black turtle beans, soaked overnight in cold water
- 4 bay leaves
- 2 large yellow onions, coarsely chopped
- ½ pound (225 g; about 3 to 4) carrots, peeled and chopped
- 3 to 4 ribs celery, sliced
- 2 tablespoons (20 g) chopped garlic
- ¼ pound (½ cup, 1 stick, or 115 g) unsalted butter
- ¼ cup (60 ml) cider or sherry vinegar
- 1 cup (235 ml) dry Madeira
- Grated zest and juice of 2 lemons
- 2 teaspoons (2.2 g) ground mace or nutmeg
- Salt and freshly ground black pepper
- 1 or 2 lemons, for garnish
- 2 hard-cooked eggs, for garnish
- 2 tablespoons (6 g) thinly sliced chives, for garnish

1. Place the ham hocks, stock, and 3 quarts (3 L) cold water into a large soup pot. Bring to a boil, skimming as necessary. Reduce heat and simmer 3 hours or until the hocks are starting to get tender.

Drain and rinse the soaked black turtle beans. Add them to the pot with the ham hocks along with the bay leaves. Bring to a boil and skim off any white foam impurities that rise to the surface. Reduce the heat and simmer for 2 hours or until the beans are starting to break apart and are soft enough to be easily mashed with a fork against the side of the pot.

2. After the beans have cooked for about 1 hour, cook the onions, carrots, celery, and garlic in the butter over medium heat until softened but not browned. Transfer the mixture to the soup pot and continue simmering until the beans are quite soft and starting to break apart.

3. Remove and discard the bay leaves and ham hocks, making sure to remove all hard bits of bone that may have fallen off the hocks.

4. In a blender or food processor, purée the soup. Take care when puréeing hot soup. To avoid hot soup splattering out of the blender jar, *do not* fill the container much more than halfway, make sure the lid is on tight, and always start at slow speed and increase as you go.

5. Strain through a food mill or sieve as shown here to remove the bean skins.

6. Press down firmly onto the bean purée using the back of a ladle to extract as much liquid as possible.

7. Return the purée to the soup pot and stir in the vinegar, Madeira, lemon zest, lemon juice, and mace.

8. Bring the soup back to a boil, skimming off any white foam that rises to the top.

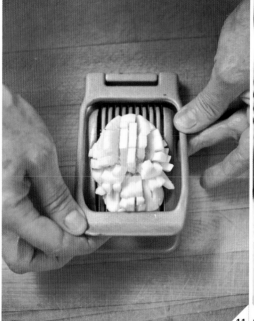

9     11 12

**9.** Prepare the garnishes: Thinly slice 1 to 2 lemons. You'll need one slice for each bowl of soup. Remove and discard any pits from the lemon slices.

**10.** Cut hard-cooked (but not fully cooked, as shown here) eggs into slices using a wire egg slicer.

**11.** Turn eggs ninety degrees, keeping the slices together, and slice again to make small strips of egg.

**12.** Thinly slice chives for garnish (see "Cutting Chives," page 97).

**13.** Season soup to taste with salt and pepper, and then pour into individual bowls. Garnish each portion with a lemon slice, chopped egg, and chives and serve immediately.

# SOUPMAKER'S TIPS

❋ Wrap the hocks in cheesecloth to make it easier to remove them once cooked, as they will start to come apart into pieces when cooked for a long time. The long cooking time for the hocks helps break down the collagen they contain, adding richness and smooth, slightly sticky mouthfeel to the soup.

❋ Substitute smoked turkey legs, wings, or neck bones if you don't eat pork. If using legs, be extra careful to remove and discard the hard bony tendons that tend to come off the legs when cooked for a long time, or wrap in cheesecloth before cooking.

**SAVE FOR STOCK:**
Ham hocks that are still intact (may be saved to use another time); trimmings of onions including skins, tops and bottoms; carrot tops and bottoms (no skins); celery trimmings; garlic skins; chive trimmings, especially tougher whitish bottom portions.

# GREEK LENTIL SOUP (Faki)

THIS DELICIOUS LENTIL SOUP, *faki* in Greek, is a popular dish during the Lenten season when meat is not eaten, so it is a traditionally vegan soup. Simple to make, with few ingredients—though each one is essential—it has full-bodied flavor and texture. Imported Greek oregano, or *rigani*, sold dried on the branch, is highly resinous with a powerful aroma and is preferred, but fresh oregano is also excellent.

**Makes 1 gallon (4 L), serves 8 to 12**

### INGREDIENTS

- 1 pound (2 cups, or 455 g) French green lentils
- 1 gallon (4 L) Vegetable Stock (page 14)
- 2 bay leaves
- 1 pound (455 g; about 1 large or 2 medium) onions, diced
- ½ pound (225 g; about 3) carrots, diced
- ¼ pound (115 g; about 3 ribs) celery, diced
- 1 pound (2 cups, or 455 g) chopped plum tomatoes, canned or fresh (if fresh, the tomatoes should be peeled and seeded)
- 3 cloves garlic, chopped (about 1 tablespoon, or 10 g)
- ½ cup (120 ml) extra-virgin olive oil
- 1 tablespoon (3 g) crumbled oregano (preferably Greek)
- Salt and freshly ground black pepper
- ¼ cup (60 ml) fresh lemon juice (about 2 lemons)
- Hot sauce, optional

Though not traditional, here we use firm French green lentils because they keep their shape and have a nutty flavor. In the European Union, the term *Le Puy Green Lentil* may only be used to designate lentils that come from the region of Le Puy in south-central France near the Loire River. Similar lentils are now also grown in the United States.

Place the lentils in a large soup pot with the Vegetable Stock and bay leaves and bring to a boil, skimming as necessary. Reduce the heat and simmer 30 minutes or until the lentils are half cooked.

**1.** Add the onions, carrots, celery, tomatoes, garlic, olive oil, and oregano. Add salt and pepper to taste. Continue cooking for 30 minutes, or until the lentils are tender but still whole and the soup is slightly thickened.

**2.** Just before serving, stir in the lemon juice.

**3.** Transfer the soup to a tureen, as here, or divide among individual soup bowls. If desired, serve with hot sauce.

Store, refrigerated up to 5 days or freeze.

**SAVE FOR STOCK:**
Onion, carrots, celery, and tomato trimmings. You may add one squeezed-out lemon shell to chicken or fish stock.

## TECHNIQUE

## Cutting Chives

The most delicate member of the onion family, chives make a beautiful garnish with a slightly sharp, oniony flavor and complement many soups, especially light-colored smooth cream soups from the French tradition, such as Lobster Bisque with Cognac, the Corn Cream Soup with Summer Vegetables, or the Green Gazpacho with Garlic, Grapes, and Almonds (pages 58, 69, 140 respectively). If picked in dry hot weather, you may need to pick through the chives and remove any dried brownish stalks. If picked in wet hot weather, you may need to pick through and remove any slimy stalks.

**1.** Line up the chives with their ends all facing the same direction and grasp the lower portion of the bundle with your nondominant hand.

**2.** Using a sharp chef's knife, slice off the top portion of the bundle and line it up next to the remaining chives to form a thicker bundle.

**3.** Again grasping the bundle with your nondominant hand and keeping it in a compact shape, slice the chives crosswise into thin slices.

**4.** Continue slicing, but keep the fingers of your nondominant hand curled so you don't cut them with the knife.

**5.** Slice until only tougher, whitish ends remain. Either save for stock or discard the ends.

# TURKISH RED LENTIL SOUP (Mercimek Çorbasi)

*MERCIMEK* MEANS "RED LENTIL" In Turkish, and *çorbasi* means "soup." Together they make one of Turkey's most basic and simple soups, quick and inexpensive to make and easy to adapt to vegetarian or vegan diets or for kosher meat meals by using vegetable stock instead of milk. The soup is flavored with spearmint, which grows profusely throughout the Mediterranean region. Ground sumac imparts tang while maroon Urfa *biber* (pepper) adds fruity heat. A few drops of paprika-infused olive oil provide the finishing touch.

**Makes about 1 gallon (4 L), serves 8 to 12**

**INGREDIENTS**

- 1 pound (2 cups, or 455 g) split red lentils
- 1 large onion, chopped
- 3 garlic cloves, minced
- 2 teaspoons (12.5 g) kosher salt
- ½ teaspoon (1 g) ground black pepper
- 3 tablespoons (17 g) chopped fresh mint, or 1 tablespoon (1.6 g) dried mint, preferably spearmint
- 3 tablespoons (48 g) tomato paste
- 1 tablespoon (3.6 g) Turkish Urfa pepper (substitute Aleppo pepper or other hot pepper flakes)
- ½ cup (120 ml) olive oil, divided
- 6 tablespoons (47 g) all-purpose flour
- 2 cups (475 ml) milk (or Vegetable Stock, page 14)
- 1 tablespoon (15 ml) paprika
- Chopped fresh mint, preferably spearmint or dried mint (see "Cutting Herb Leaves into Chiffonade," page 100), for garnish
- Ground sumac (see "Soupmaker's Tips" on page 99), for garnish
- 1 lemon, cut in thick half-moon wedges, for garnish

1. Rinse and drain the red lentils. They will absorb a little of the water and expand.

2. In a large pot, mix red lentils, onion, garlic, salt, black pepper, mint, tomato paste, and Urfa pepper.

3. Add 3 quarts (3 L) of water to the pot and bring to a boil. Skim off the foam that rises to the top. Reduce the heat and simmer half an hour or until the lentils have disintegrated, stirring occasionally.

4. Meanwhile, in a small pot, combine ¼ cup (60 ml) olive oil and flour to make a smooth paste. Cook 3 to 5 minutes, stirring, to cook out the raw flour. Add the milk (or Vegetable Stock) while whisking or stirring vigorously and bring to a boil, stirring until smooth.

5. Scrape the mixture into the soup and bring back to boil. Taste soup for seasoning and reserve.

6. Make the paprika oil garnish: Heat the remaining oil in a small skillet and then add the paprika, stirring and cooking 5 to 10 seconds.

7. Divide the soup among individual soup bowls. Drizzle some paprika oil onto each bowl and sprinkle mint and sumac just before serving.

8. Add a wedge of lemon to each bowl and serve.

# SOUPMAKER'S TIPS

❖ Buy inexpensive red lentils at an Indian grocery and store refrigerated or frozen, especially in hot weather months. Keep a bag on hand to make this 30-minute soup.

❖ This soup will thicken a lot as it stands. When reheating, pour a thin layer of water onto the bottom of the pot and then add the soup so it doesn't stick. Stir often when reheating.

❖ Like most bean soups, this soup freezes perfectly, so double the recipe and freeze half in quart-size freezer containers or sturdy deli containers. (Look for deli containers that are reinforced at the rim— they are sturdier and you'll be able to reuse them several times.)

### SAVE FOR STOCK:
Onion trimmings, garlic trimmings

### SUMAC:
Sumac spice comes from the dark burgundy-red fruits of *Rhus coriaria* and is unrelated to poison sumac. The small fruits are dried and ground to a coarse, moist texture. It has a fruity, tangy aroma and lemony-tart, resinous flavor with a salty aftertaste from the salt included as a preservative. Sumac bushes grow wild in the Mediterranean and are found in Lebanon, Syria, Egypt, and Turkey.

### URFA PEPPER:
Urfa pepper (*biber* in Turkish) is a special maroon chile grown in the Urfa region of Eastern Turkey then dried and ground in a complex method. It has a distinctive smoky, dried fruit flavor, and mild but lasting heat. Look for Urfa pepper in Middle Eastern markets or from specialty spice stores. The closest substitute is dried ancho chiles from Mexico.

# Cutting Herb Leaves into Chiffonade

To cut into *chiffonade* is to slice green leaves into narrow strips. You may use this technique to cut large herb leaves such as mint, basil, cilantro, or parsley, but not thyme, tarragon, or rosemary, which have narrow, needlelike leaves.

**1.** Wash and drain the spearmint, the preferred culinary variety in North Africa, Turkey, and the Eastern Mediterranean. Note that some hothouse-grown mint will lack flavor and aroma. Dried spearmint, purchased in whole leaf form as *nana* from a Middle Eastern market, or the contents of mint tea bags may be substituted.

**2.** Gather the mint into a compact bundle, then, using a sharp chef's knife, slice across to make narrow strips, or chiffonade, of mint. The sharper the knife, the cleaner the cut, and the longer the mint (or other herb) will keep its appealing green color. A dull knife will yield oxidized (brownish) strips.

To store washed and drained or cut herb leaves, roll them into paper towels and place them into a plastic ziplock bag. If the leaves are totally dry, dampen the paper towels first. Once cut, the strips will quickly deteriorate, so use them within 1 day.

# PASTA E FAGIOLI

THIS PEASANT SOUP IS BASED ON inexpensive, hearty, substantial beans in broth thickened with pasta and is found throughout Italy. The texture of this soup ranges from thin and smooth if puréed to thick and hearty, almost stewlike, depending on region and taste. In this recipe, we use pancetta (pork belly that has been salt and air-cured like prosciutto) for its potent savory flavor and rich fat, but you may substitute more olive oil. Pasta e Fagioli is often made with tender-skinned cannellini (white kidney) beans or meaty borlotti (or Romano) beans. Better yet is to use fresh shelled beans such as cranberry beans (found in season at farmers' markets and Asian groceries), which don't need any soaking. You will need to start the soup one day ahead to soak the beans. This soup freezes well without the pasta. Add the pasta after reheating the soup.

**Makes about 1 gallon (4 L), serves 8 to 12**

### INGREDIENTS

- ½ pound (225 g) pancetta, chilled until firm (see "Soupmaker's Tips," page 51)
- ¼ cup (60 ml) extra-virgin olive oil, plus 2 tablespoons (30 ml) for serving
- 1 small red onion, chopped
- ½ fennel bulb, finely chopped
- 3 carrots, finely diced
- 3 ribs celery, thinly sliced
- 1 tablespoon (10 g) chopped garlic
- 2 cups (360 g) chopped plum tomatoes (canned or fresh)
- 6 cups (600 g) cooked cannellini beans (see "Cooking Dried Beans," pafge 103)
- 2 quarts (2 L) Chicken or Vegetable Stock (page 9 or 14)
- ½ pound (225 g) ditalini or small dried pasta shells
- 2 cups (40 g) whole baby arugula or large arugula leaves shredded (if field-grown, wash the arugula thoroughly)
- Sea salt and freshly ground black pepper
- 2 ounces (55 g) each grated Parmigiano-Reggiano and Romano cheeses

Baby arugula is prewashed and easy to use in this soup but larger field-grown arugula works as well. Just be sure to wash it thoroughly, changing the water if necessary. Slice larger leaves of arugula crosswise into 1-inch (2.5 cm) sections before adding to the soup.

1 2 5

8 9 10 11

**1.** Use a sharp chef's knife to slice all around the outside as a cutting guide. Following the guide, slice off a piece of pancetta about 1-inch (2.5 cm) thick, which will weigh about ½ pound (225 g).

**2.** Cut the pancetta into small cubes by first slicing into ¼-inch (6 mm) slices. Then cut the slices into thick sticks.

**3.** Turn the sticks around so the ends are facing the knife. Cut the sticks into cubes.

**4.** In a large, heavy-bottomed pan, lightly brown the pancetta in the olive oil over moderate heat.

**5.** Add the red onion, fennel, carrot, celery, and garlic and cook until the vegetables are soft but not browned, about 5 minutes.

**6.** Add the tomatoes and bring to a boil.

**7.** Add the cooked beans, any bean cooking liquid, and the Chicken Stock and bring back to a boil.

**8.** Reduce the heat, and simmer 30 minutes, stirring occasionally, or until the beans are quite tender.

**9.** Remove about one-fourth of the bean mixture from the pot and blend to a creamy purée. Return to the pot.

Meanwhile, bring a large pot of salted water to a boil. Add the pasta and cook until firm to the bite (about 8 minutes). Drain, reserving 1 cup (235 ml) of the pasta cooking water.

Add the pasta and reserved pasta cooking water (which helps bind the soup due to the starch it contains) to the soup and stir to combine (see "Soupmaker's Tips").

**10.** Just before serving, stir in the arugula, the salt and pepper to taste, and then let the mixture rest for 5 minutes.

**11.** Ladle into soup bowls or a tureen and sprinkle with the grated cheese.

**12.** Drizzle each portion with extra virgin olive oil.

**13.** Serve the soup.

# SOUPMAKER'S TIPS

❊ If you're planning to serve the soup more than once, add only enough of the cooked pasta for each portion. As the pasta sits in the broth it will continue to absorb liquid and will become soft and mushy. To avoid this, run cold water onto the cooked pasta, drain well, and then toss with a little olive oil. Reserve chilled until you're ready to serve the soup.

**SAVE FOR STOCK:**
Fennel stalks and outer leaves, celery trimmings, garlic skins and trimmings, tomato trimmings if using fresh tomatoes (don't use red onion trimmings, which will darken stock)

# Cooking Dried Beans

When cooking dried beans, it's important to cook them as slowly as possible so they keep their shape. Soaking the beans overnight and discarding the soaking water allows them to cook more evenly because they've already been hydrated. In addition, soaking and discarding the water also helps with digestion. You may take one further step (especially if you suspect the beans are old): After soaking and draining the beans, cover them with cold water and bring to a boil. Cook for 5 minutes, then drain, discarding the water, and then continue with the first step.

**Makes about 6 cups (600 g) cooked beans**

- 1 pound (455 g) dried beans
- 1 whole onion, peeled and stuck with 4 whole cloves (see Appendix, page 148)
- ½ head garlic, excess outer skin rubbed off, ½ inch (1 cm) sliced off the top to expose the cloves
- 2 bay leaves
- 1 whole dried red chile pepper (optional), substitute 1 teaspoon (1.2 g) hot red pepper flakes

1

Place the beans in a bowl, cover with 1 quart (1 L) cold water and soak overnight or until plump and fully hydrated. Drain and rinse the beans.

**1.** Transfer beans to a medium-sized pot. Add 1½ quarts (1.5 L) cold water, bring to a boil, skimming off and discarding the white foam protein impurities that rise to the top. Simmer 2 hours or until the beans are almost completely tender, shaking the pot occasionally so the beans don't stick to the bottom.

**2.** Add the whole onion, garlic, bay leaves, and (optional) hot pepper and bring back to a boil.

**3.** Remove from the heat, remove and discard the onion, garlic, bay leaves, and chile pepper, and reserve. Cool without stirring, to avoid breaking up the beans, and then drain.

Once cooled, you may freeze cooked beans to add later to soups such as Acquacotta Maremmana, page 83.

# Chapter 7
# HEARTY SOUPS

These inexpensive, bountiful soups are main dish meals that inspire contentment.

IN THIS CHAPTER ARE HEARTY SOUPS, substantial and chunky, containing small pieces of meats, vegetables, legumes, and grains, somewhere between a liquid soup and a thick stew. They are usually served in cold weather when that big pot can stay on the stove for hours helping to heat the room and warm us up on the inside. Because this category of soups is made with a long list of ingredients, they are difficult to make in small quantities. Most freeze well, so get out your biggest pot and start chopping.

Here we find international specialties such as Vietnamese Pho Soup with Beef Brisket (page 109) with its French influence. The vegan Creole Gumbo Z'Herbes (page 106) comes from Creole Louisiana traditions but has a strong African influence. The Mexican Sopa de Tortilla with Shredded Chicken (page 115) is a great way of using up stale tortillas and is fresh tasting with its slew of garnishes. The toasted chiles in the soup are dried and may be kept in the pantry. The Portuguese Caldo Verde (page 113), or "hot green" soup, is full of shredded kale and the spicy Portuguese pork sausage called *chouriço*. Caldo gallego is a related soup from Galicia in northern Spain made with white beans and kale. The Rumanian Beet-Vegetable Borscht with Beef Brisket (page 119) is best made in fall and winter when the root vegetables it calls for are in season. A last minute addition of brown sugar and lemon provide a palate-awakening sweet-tart flavor.

Other hearty soups include the whole family of Italian minestrone—a *minestra* is a simple soup with few ingredients, a *minestrone* is a complex soup with lots of ingredients, and closely related to the Acquacotta Maremmana (page 83). Its French cousin is *soupe au pistou*, a mix of summer vegetables including Swiss chard, and topped with a tomato or basil pistou. *Garbure*, from Gascony in Southwestern France, is a country-style cabbage soup containing ham or the local specialty of preserved meats such as confit of duck. Fava beans, potatoes, turnips, kohlrabi, chestnuts, nettles, and borage leaves may show up in the pot.

A *potée* is an ancient French dish usually including preserved pork, root vegetables, and sauerkraut. Dutch and Flemish *hutspot* is a filling dish of root vegetables that may be boiled and mashed or served in a broth with meat, especially beef. This very old term, which can be translated as "shaken pot," is a cousin to English *hotchpot* and French *hochepot*, substantial stews of meat and barley. The term evolved into *hodge-podge*, a jumbled mixture.

Spanish *cocido*, which invariably contains chickpeas, is simmered in a large pot and is related to Italian *bollito misto*, and even the traditional New England boiled dinner, all of which contain a variety of meats and hearty root vegetables cooked in a rich broth. These dishes may be served in multiple courses with the vegetables first, the cooked meats second, and the broth third. Cocido often has fine noodles added to it just before serving. Bollito misto is accompanied by various highly seasoned sauces and condiments for the meats. Robust bean soups like Italian pasta e fagioli and chunky Cuban-style black bean soup also fall into this category.

These slow-cooked, hearty soups are perfect family fare—inexpensive, substantial, and full of rounded flavor. They are usually served in large bowls as the main dish of the meal, accompanied by crusty bread for dunking and perhaps followed by a green salad.

# CREOLE GUMBO Z'HERBES

GUMBO Z'HERBES, a soupy stew of slow-cooked greens, is traditionally served on Good Friday during Lent in Creole country—southeastern Louisiana. Many recipes call for seven different cooking greens for good luck. Gumbo originated in southern Louisiana during the eighteenth century and consists of a rich broth, a thickener, and aromatic vegetables such as celery, bell peppers, and onion—the Creole kitchen's "holy trinity." This gumbo is thickened with a dark roux, paste of deeply browned flour and fat. We use oil rather than butter, because this is a soup for Lent when no animal foods are served. Gumbo gets its name either from the Bantu word for okra (*ki ngombo*) or the Choctaw word for filé or ground sassafras leaf, (*kombo*). This soup is suitable for vegans and vegetarians, and it freezes well.

**Makes 1 gallon (4 L), serves about 12**

### INGREDIENTS

- 5 bunches assorted cooking greens, such as spinach, collards, kale, watercress, curly endive, and chicory; mustard, turnips, beets, carrots, and radish tops; and arugula
- ¾ cup (175 ml) olive oil
- 1 cup (126 g) all-purpose flour
- 2 bunches scallions, white and light green parts thinly sliced; reserve green tops for garnish
- 1 medium yellow onion, diced
- 1 large green bell pepper, diced
- 4 celery stalks, diced
- 2 tablespoons (20 g) minced garlic
- Salt and pepper
- 2 quarts (2 L) Vegetable Stock (page 14)
- 2 bay leaves
- 6 sprigs fresh thyme, tied with kitchen string (see Appendix, page 149)
- ½ teaspoon cayenne pepper
- 1 bunch parsley, leaves and tender stems chopped
- ½ teaspoon ground allspice
- ¼ teaspoon ground cloves
- 3 tablespoons (45 ml) cider vinegar, plus additional for serving
- ½ cup (83 g) cooked white rice per person, for serving
- Hot sauce, for serving

Rinse and trim the greens, removing any dried-out parts, wilted, slimy, or broken leaves, and tough stems that don't break easily. If you're using collards and kale, remove the tough inner rib that runs up the center of each leaf.

Fill the sink with cold water and submerge all the greens. Leave undisturbed for about 5 minutes, and then scoop from the water and place in a colander. (Don't drain the sink with the greens still in it: Soaking the greens allows all the sand and grit to settle to the bottom of the sink—if you drain it, your greens are left sitting in the silty stuff.) If the bowl contains more than a few specks of sand, repeat the process. (Don't ruin a whole pot of soup with sandy greens.)

**1.** Cut the greens into ½- to 1-inch (1 to 2.5 cm) thick ribbons.

**2.** Transfer greens to a large pot with a tight-fitting lid. Add water to fill the pot about halfway. Season generously with salt. Cover and cook over medium-high heat. When the water in the pot begins to simmer, cover tightly and reduce the heat to medium low.

**3.** Cook the greens, occasionally turning with a pair of tongs or a spoon, until they are very soft and wilted, 30 to 40 minutes. Strain the greens, making sure to reserve the cooking liquid. (You should have about 1 quart, or 1 liter.) Allow the greens to cool slightly.

**4.** Working in two to three batches, place a portion of the greens into a blender (preferable for finer texture) or the bowl of a food processor. (You will process about half of the greens.)

**5.** Add a ladleful of the reserved cooking liquid to each batch in the blender.

**6.** Blend the greens to a thick purée that still has some chunky texture. Mix the puréed greens with the remaining half of the cooked, sliced greens, and reserve.

**7.** Now prepare the roux: In a large, heavy-bottomed pot or Dutch oven, heat the olive oil over medium heat. Slowly sprinkle in the flour and stir to combine into a thick, smooth paste.

**8.** Cook while stirring the roux constantly with a wooden spoon or wire whisk to prevent lumps from forming.

9

10

11 12

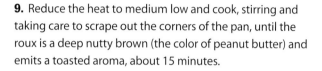

14 15

**9.** Reduce the heat to medium low and cook, stirring and taking care to scrape out the corners of the pan, until the roux is a deep nutty brown (the color of peanut butter) and emits a toasted aroma, about 15 minutes.

**10.** Preferably use a wooden spoon or silicone spatula to stir in the scallions, onion, bell pepper, celery, and garlic. Season generously with salt and freshly ground black pepper.

**11.** Cook, stirring often, until the vegetables are softened but not browned, about 5 minutes.

**12.** Add the reserved greens cooking liquid, along with the Vegetable Stock and the reserved puréed and sliced greens.

**13.** Add the bay leaves, thyme bundle, cayenne pepper, parsley, allspice, and cloves, and stir well to combine.

**14.** Increase the heat to medium high and bring the soup mixture to a light boil. Reduce heat and simmer, stirring often, until the gumbo base is soupy and thick and the vegetables are tender, about 15 minutes.

Simmer the gumbo 10 minutes to meld the flavors, stirring often so it doesn't stick and burn. Remove from the heat and stir in the vinegar.

**15.** Ladle the soup around a mound of cooked white rice in individual serving bowls.

**16.** Sprinkle each portion with reserved scallions. Each diner can add more vinegar and hot sauce to taste.

## SOUPMAKER'S TIPS

❋ Choose a large variety of greens: some peppery, such as watercress and mustard; some biting, such as arugula; some mild, such as spinach, carrot tops, and kale; some bitter, such as chicory, turnip, and curly endive; and some aromatic, such as parsley and thyme.

❋ When making a roux, the longer you cook it, the more it darkens, but the less its thickening power. So, a soup made with a dark roux will require more roux than one made with an ordinary blond roux.

**SAVE FOR STOCK:**
Scallion root ends; onion, green pepper, and celery trimmings; thyme and parsley stems.

# VIETNAMESE PHO SOUP WITH BEEF BRISKET

PHO IS A VIETNAMESE rice noodle soup traditionally served in beef broth. It originated in the North Vietnamese capital of Hanoi, which had an important textile market where the soup was sold by vendors from large boxes. The first restaurant specializing in pho opened in the 1920s, but the soup is still a popular street food often eaten at night. It is possible that the word *pho* derives from the French *pot-au-feu* (fire) that originated during the period of French colonial rule. After the Vietnam War, refugees fled to

U.S. cities where they opened restaurants specializing in pho with a choice of tough, flavorful beef cuts such as brisket and flank or meatballs. Northern Vietnamese pho tends to use wider noodles and more scallions; southern Vietnamese pho, like this one, is sweeter and includes bean sprouts, abundant fresh herbs, and fish sauce. Here, fresh mint, cilantro, bean sprouts, limes, green chiles, scallions, hoisin, and Sriracha sauce are added to the soup by each diner according to taste.

**Makes about 1 gallon (4 L), serves 10 to 12**

### INGREDIENTS

- 3 quarts (3 L) Vietnamese Beef Broth (recipe follows)
- 2 to 3 pounds (907 g to 1.4 kg) brisket of beef (with or without fat)
- 1 package (6 ounces, or 168 g) thin rice noodles (*mai fun*)
- ¼ pound (115 g) snow pea pods
- 1 pint (100 g) mung bean sprouts
- 1 bunch cilantro, leaves picked off
- 1 bunch Thai holy basil (or ½ bunch sweet basil plus ½ bunch mint)
- 1 bunch scallions, sliced on the bias into ½-inch (1 cm) sections
- 2 limes, cut into wedges
- 2 to 3 jalapeno peppers, thinly sliced
- ¼ cup (60 ml) Sriracha Thai hot sauce
- ¼ cup (60 ml) Chinese Hoisin sauce

Place the broth in a soup pot, add the brisket and bring to a boil. Simmer 3 hours, or until the brisket is tender when pierced with a skewer or fork but still holds its shape.

**1.** Remove the brisket (here a whole brisket, with its fat and both upper flat and lower point muscles) from the pot and cool covered with damp paper towels to prevent a skin from forming. Reserve the broth.

**2.** Trim off any fat from the outside and discard.

**3.** Here we trim the spongy fat and connective tissue between the two layers of muscle.

**4.** Trimmed brisket ready to slice.

**5.** Slice the brisket as thinly as possible against the grain and reserve.

**6.** Place the rice noodles in a large bowl and cover with cold water. Allow the noodles to soften until pliable, about 20 minutes.

**7.** Meanwhile, add the sliced brisket to the pot and bring back to a boil.

**8.** Add the pea pods and bean sprouts to the pot and stir to combine.

**9.** Place the cilantro and basil leaves into the bottom of individual serving bowls. Add a handful of drained, softened rice noodles to each bowl.

**10.** Ladle the soup broth over top.

**11.** Place scallions, lime wedges, sliced jalapenos, Sriracha sauce, and Hoisin sauce in small bowls. Diners can add their choice of the garnishes to their bowl and then ladle in the hot soup.

# VIETNAMESE BEEF BROTH

Make the Vietnamese Beef Broth ahead of time, freezing if desired.

### Makes about 3 quarts (3 L)

#### INGREDIENTS

- 3 pounds (1.4 kg) oxtail, cut by the butcher in 1-inch (2.5 cm) sections
- 3 pounds (1.4 kg) beef shin, cut by the butcher in 1-inch (2.5 cm) sections
- 1 onion, unpeeled and cut in quarters
- 1 piece (3 inch, or 7.5 cm) fresh ginger, cut in half lengthwise
- 6 whole cloves
- 8 whole star anise pods
- 2 cinnamon sticks
- 4 bay leaves
- 1 tablespoon (5.8 g) fennel seeds

Preheat the oven to 400°F (200°C, or gas mark 6). Place the oxtail and beef shin in a roasting pan just large enough to hold them. Roast until brown, about 1½ hours, turn bones so they roast evenly and cook until deep brown, about 30 minutes longer.

Transfer the contents of the roasting to a stock pot, scraping out any browned bits from the pan. Cover with 1 gallon (4 L) cold water and bring to a boil. Skim off any foam that rises to the top, which will be white at the beginning and then light tan. Continue to skim until the broth is mostly clear. Reduce the heat to a simmer.

Meanwhile, place a cast-iron or steel skillet over high heat. When the skillet is hot, add the onion and ginger halves and cook till charred on all sides. Then, add the remaining ingredients to the broth, including the onion and ginger. Simmer at the lowest possible heat at least 8 hours, or until the meat falls to pieces.

Strain the broth, discarding the solids. Refrigerate the broth overnight or until the fat solidifies on top. Remove the fat and discard, reserving the broth. If you are pressed for time, you can skip the cooling process but remove as much fat as possible using a ladle.

# SOUPMAKER'S TIPS

❋ The beef broth freezes quite well and will keep about 5 days refrigerated, so make it ahead of time. Otherwise, allow 24 hours to make the soup from start to finish.

❋ If you don't have time to wait for the broth to chill thoroughly so the fat solidifies, you may remove the last bit of fat from the top of the broth by laying paper towels on the surface, which will absorb the fat. Repeat once.

❋ Brisket of beef comes from the front of the "breast" of the cow and includes two distinct muscles: the larger, pointed oblong-shaped lean flat, or first cut, and the smaller, fattier triangular second cut, attached together by a thick layer of spongy fat and connective tissue. While brisket is prized for its robust beefy flavor, it must be cooked slowly at low heat, shrinking by about half its weight during cooking. The brisket flat is commonly sold on its own and includes little to no fat; the second cut is sold as part of a whole brisket either on or off the bone. Look for brisket at markets catering to an eastern European Jewish clientele or in Texas, where it's the preferred cut for Texas-style barbecue.

❋ Sriracha is a thickened red sauce made from hot red chiles, vinegar, garlic, sugar, and salt, and it's named after the coastal city of Si Racha in central Thailand. In Thailand, Sriracha is a dipping sauce for seafood; in Vietnam, Sriracha is a condiment for pho and spring rolls. In the United States, Rooster brand dominates the market, and the sauce is served at many restaurants, from diners to burger joints.

❋ Dark brown, thick and sweet, hoisin sauce comes from Peking, China, and includes starches such as sweet potato, wheat or rice, and toasted, mashed soybeans, along with sugar, vinegar, salt, garlic, and red chiles.

**SAVE FOR STOCK:**

If desired, reserve the simmered beef shank and shin and brisket trimmings to make a second stock. Known as *remouillage* (rewetting) in French, the second cooking will produce a light-bodied stock that nevertheless has good beef flavor when combined with other ingredients.

Save snow pea trimmings, cilantro stems (use in stock for Asian and Latin American soups), basil stems (mint stems are quite strong and can be simmered in sugar syrup to make a mint-infused syrup suitable for sweetening iced tea, cocktails, and fruit macedoine). Use ginger peelings and trimmings the same way. Save light-colored scallion trimmings—discard the dark green tops as these will dye the stock an unpleasant grayish green.

# PORTUGUESE CALDO VERDE

*CALDO VERDE*, WHICH MEANS "hot green broth," is considered by many to be Portugal's national dish. This kale-based soup originated in the Minho Province in northern Portugal but has become a national favorite found everywhere from fancy hotel dining rooms to humble peasant homes. The kale used in Portugal, known as *Tronchuda*, has large, paddle-shaped dark blue-green leaves with thick, white, fleshy ribs and mild, sweet flavor and is sometimes substituted by collard greens. Caldo Verde is often accompanied by *broa*, yeast-raised Portuguese cornbread, for sopping up the delicious juices— similar to American Southern soul food in which sweetened cornbread sops up "pot liquor," the cooking juices of simmered collard greens.

**Makes about 5 quarts (5 L), serves 10 to 12**

### INGREDIENTS

- ¼ cup (60 ml) extra-virgin olive oil
- ½ pound (225 g) chorizo sausage, sliced or cut into smaller pieces
- 1 large onion, diced
- 3 quarts (3 L) Chicken Stock (page 9), simmering
- 2 pounds (907 g) potatoes, preferably gold such as Yukon Gold, quartered and sliced
- 3 cloves garlic, minced
- Salt and fresh ground black pepper
- 1 large bunch kale, leaves shredded

1  5

3

## SOUPMAKER'S TIPS

❈ You may use Spanish-style dry-cured chorizo, Mexican style fresh chorizo, or authentic Portuguese *chouriço* here. All three are made from pork but Spanish chorizo is often smoked and dry-cured. It is seasoned with wine or garlic and with sweet and hot Spanish paprika. Mexican chorizo is a fresh sausage and must be cooked. Chouriço is a closely related Portuguese wood-smoked sausage seasoned with sweet paprika, garlic, salt, white or red wine, and Angolan *piri-piri* (hot pepper sauce).

❈ Though Caldo Verde is often made with Vegetable Stock or simply water for the liquid, the richness and body of Chicken Stock make the soup more substantial and flavorful.

**SAVE FOR STOCK:**
Onion trimmings, potato trimmings (don't save kale stems as cole—cabbage family—vegetables lend a disagreeably strong flavor to stock)

**1.** Place olive oil in a large soup pot—here a French-style rondeau—and heat. Add the sausage and brown while breaking up the sausage into small bits.

**2.** Add the onions and cook over medium heat or until softened but not browned.

**3.** Add the Chicken Stock and use a wooden spoon to release the tasty browned bits on the bottom of the pot.

**4.** Add the potatoes, the garlic, and the salt and pepper to taste. Bring to a boil, and then lower the heat and simmer until potatoes are half cooked, about 10 minutes.

**5.** Add the shredded kale to the soup and cook until tender, about 25 minutes.

**6.** Taste for seasoning and serve.

# MEXICAN SOPA DE TORTILLA WITH SHREDDED CHICKEN

MADE IN INNUMERABLE VERSIONS, this substantial soup (also known as *Sopa Azteca*) is tangy with lime juice and spicy hot from toasted guajillo, and it was developed as a frugal cook's way to use up stale tortillas. It is garnished at the table with toasted pasilla chiles, crunchy fried tortilla strips, cilantro—though some people use stronger epazote—mild queso fresco (substitute mild feta or halloumi cheese), and buttery sliced avocado. Though chicken broth is most common, Smoked Turkey Stock adds robust flavor. The soup base freezes well but the garnishes must be prepared fresh.

**Makes 3 quarts (3 L), serves 8 to 12**

### INGREDIENTS

- 4 dried guajillo chiles
- 2 dried pasilla chiles, stemmed
- 3 quarts (3 L) Chicken Stock, Roasted Chicken Broth, or Smoked Turkey Stock (page 9, 20, or 11), divided
- ¾ pound (340 g) boneless skinless chicken thighs
- 2 tablespoons (30 ml) vegetable oil
- 1 small onion, diced
- 2 cloves garlic, minced
- 2 teaspoons (5 g) ground cumin
- Crunchy Fried Tortilla Strips (see "Crunchy Fried Tortilla Strips," page 118) divided
- 2 cups (360 g) chopped plum tomatoes, fresh or canned (if using fresh, remove the skins)
- ½ bunch cilantro, leaves and tender stems picked off for garnish
- Juice of 4 key limes, substitute the juice of 2 limes, plus extra juice and limes for garnish
- Kosher salt
- ¼ pound (115 g) queso fresco, crumbled
- 2 firm but ripe avocados, sliced (see Appendix, page 152)

1. Cut off the stem ends of the guajillo and pasilla chiles.

2. Cut down the sides of the chiles.

3. Open up the chiles, exposing the seeds.

4. Shake out the seeds and discard them.

5. Use scissors or a knife to slice the pasilla chiles into thin strips and reserve.

6. Heat a large heavy skillet, preferably cast iron, until just beginning to smoke. Add the guajillo chiles, pressing down with a spatula to flatten them and cook briefly, just until the chiles begin to smoke. Remove from the skillet and reserve for the soup broth.

Repeat with the pasilla chile strips. Cut the pasilla chiles crosswise into thin strips and reserve for garnish.

Meanwhile, in a medium pot, heat 2 cups (475 ml) of the stock or broth. Add the chicken thighs and bring the liquid to a boil, skimming off any white foam. Reduce the heat, cover, and simmer until the chicken is firm, about 15 minutes.

7. Allow the chicken thighs to cool in the broth, and then drain, reserving the broth and the chicken.

8. Slice the chicken thinly against the grain and reserve.

9. In a large soup pot, heat the oil, add the onion, garlic, cumin, and crumbled toasted guajillo chiles and cook until the onions are soft and tender but not browned, about 5 minutes.

10. Add about one-third of the fried tortilla strips and the tomatoes and stir to combine.

11. Add the reserved chicken poaching broth and the remaining broth or stock, here robust Smoked Turkey Stock (page 11).

**12.** Bring to a boil. Reduce heat, cover, and simmer until liquid has mostly been absorbed and chiles are soft, stirring occasionally, about 15 minutes.

**13.** Working in batches, blend the mixture in the jar of a blender or using an immersion blender until smooth. Pour the puréed mixture back into the soup pot. Add the lime juice and salt to taste and bring back to a boil.

**14.** Prepare the garnishes, clockwise from the center top: fried tortilla strips, toasted pasilla chile strips, lime juice and cut limes, crumbled queso fresco, cilantro, sliced chicken, and, in the center, sliced avocado.

The lime juice and sliced chicken are usually added to the soup pot—the other ingredients are added to taste to individual portions of the soup.

# SOUPMAKER'S TIPS

✳ An inexpensive Chinese brass wire and bamboo skimmer, also known as a spider, is best for scooping deep-fried foods from cooking oil. The brass wire repels oil so that the foods will be lighter. Almost any Asian market will sell them for about five dollars.

✳ Queso fresco is a very mild, lightly salted unaged white cheese popular in Spain, Portugal, Mexico, and Central and Latin America. It can be compared to Indian paneer, Cypriot halloumi, and mild feta and like them, it crumbles easily and in most versions, doesn't melt into creamy threads when heated.

**SAVE FOR STOCK:**
Onion trimmings, chicken thigh trimmings, fresh tomato trimmings, cilantro stems (good for Asian and Latin American soups, cilantro roots, if included, are prized in Southeast Asian cuisine for curry paste)

TECHNIQUE

# Crunchy Fried Tortilla Strips

While you can use store-bought fried tortillas here, the homemade version from fresh tortillas will be nutty, crunchy, and full of distinctive, slightly acrid nixtamalized corn flavor. Nixtamalization is a process for preparing corn in which the kernels are soaked and then cooked in an alkaline solution, usually limewater, and then hulled. Corn treated in this manner can be ground more easily, has increased nutritional value, and mycotoxins from mold and fungus are reduced. Nixtamalized corn is used to make tortillas, masa harina flour for tamales and other corn products, corn chips, and hominy or posole.

**Makes about 4 cups (245 g)**

- 1 package (12 ounces, or 340 g) corn tortillas
- 2 cups (475 ml) canola or vegetable oil, for frying

**1.** Cut the tortillas in half and then cut crosswise into strips.

Heat oil in a medium heavy pot, a wok, or a cast iron skillet. (Fill the pot no more than two-thirds full with oil.) Heat until the oil is shimmering and quite hot (see "Checking the Temperature of Frying Oil without Using a Thermometer," page 92, for how to tell when the oil is hot enough.)

**2.** Add the tortilla strips a few at a time to the pot so the temperature doesn't drop and so they don't stick together. Fry, stirring so they cook evenly, until crisp and lightly browned, about 2 minutes.

**3.** Scoop the tortilla strips from the oil using tongs, wire spider, or slotted spoon.

**4.** Drain on a wire cooling rack placed over a baking tray or on paper towels.

# RUMANIAN BEET-VEGETABLE BORSCHT WITH BEEF BRISKET

ROMANIA IS KNOWN for its large variety of vegetable dishes including this version of borscht, which contains a whole garden of vegetables—onion, carrots, parsnip, green cabbage, celery, green pepper, and tomato, and plenty of chopped dill. Today, it is the ruby-red beet root that defines borscht, but its name comes from the Russian word for cow parsnip, a root vegetable in the carrot family and presumably the soup's original base. Serve the borscht with a dollop of bright white sour cream floating on top for a meal in a bowl that tastes as good as it looks. Some cooks add finely shredded raw beets just before serving to brighten the color; others prefer to finish the soup with a few tablespoons (ml) of bottled beet concentrate, available at Russian and Eastern European markets. Allow about 6 hours from start to finish to make this soup, although most of that time is unattended. This hearty soup freezes beautifully.

**Makes about 1 gallon (4 L), serves 8 to 12**

### INGREDIENTS

- 1 pound (455 g) meaty beef bones (neck or shank)
- Salt
- 2 pounds (907 g) beef brisket (or other tough, flavorful cut used for pot roast, such as chuck, bottom round, or boneless short ribs)
- 1 large onion, thinly sliced
- ½ pound (225 g) carrots, peeled and finely diced or coarsely grated
- 1 pound (455 g) beets, peeled and finely diced or coarsely grated
- ½ pound (225 g) parsnips, peeled and finely diced or coarsely grated
- 1 small green cabbage, cored and finely shredded (substitute brussels sprouts)
- 3 ribs celery with leaves, thinly sliced
- 1 green pepper, seeded and diced
- 1 can (28 ounces, or 794 g) tomato purée
- ¼ cup (60 ml) beet concentrate (purchased) or 1 small raw beet, peeled and finely grated or processed (optional)
- Juice of 2 lemons (about ¼ cup, or 60 ml)
- ½ cup (26 g) chopped dill (about ½ bunch), divided
- ¼ cup (38 g) dark brown sugar
- Fresh ground black pepper
- ½ cup (115 g) sour cream, for garnish

Ingredients for hearty beef borscht with beets and other colorful vegetables

**1.** Place bones in a soup pot with cold water to cover by about 2 inches (5 cm). Add salt to taste, bring to a boil, and simmer for 3 hours.

**2.** Skim off the foam protein impurities that rise to the top. At first they will be white in color; as the broth cooks, the color will change to tan.

**3.** Add the brisket and 6 quarts (6 L) cold water.

**4.** Bring to a boil and continue to skim off the foam. Simmer uncovered about 1½ hours, or until the brisket is close to tender when pierced.

**5.** Scoop out the beef bones and the brisket and cool. (Save the beef bones in the freezer for use in another stock.)

**6.** When cool, trim off the outer fat layer from the brisket.

**7.** Use a boning knife to trim away any remaining fat and tough connective tissue from the brisket.

**8.** Cut the beef into slices, about ⅓-inch (1 cm) thick.

**9.** Cut the slices into sticks, about ⅓-inch (1 cm) thick.

**10.** Cut the sticks into small cubes. Reserve.

**11.** Strain broth through a fine wire chinois, as shown, or through a dampened paper towel set into a sieve, discarding the scum remaining in the sieve.

12      13      14      15   17

**12.** Pour the strained broth into a second (or the cleaned first) pot, leaving behind and discarding the last ½ to 1 cup (120 to 235 ml) of liquid, which will contain a lot of sediment.

**13.** Add the reserved cubed beef, onion, carrots, beets, parsnips, cabbage, celery, green pepper, and tomato purée.

**14.** Bring the soup to a boil, skimming as needed. Reduce the heat and simmer, partially covered, until the beef and vegetables are tender, about 30 minutes.

**15.** To brighten the color of the soup (the beet tends to turn orange after cooking), add the beet concentrate or the grated beet, if desired.

Add the lemon juice, most of the chopped dill, the dark brown sugar, and pepper to taste.

**16.** Top the borscht with a dollop of sour cream and sprinkle of chopped dill.

**17.** If brussels sprouts are in season, here shown on the branch that they spiral around when growing, substitute them for all or part of the cabbage. To prepare, trim off the tough bottoms from each sprout and then slice or cut into quarters.

# SOUPMAKER'S TIPS

❋ Wear rubber or food-safe gloves when working with beets to prevent your hands from turning beet red.

❋ When adding water to any stock or soup, it is preferable to use cold tap water, not hot because hot water is more likely to leach the heavy metal from your plumbing pipes. Using lead to solder pipes wasn't banned in the United States until 1986, and brass plumbing parts may also contain small amounts of lead. Because of that, the U.S. EPA (Environmental Protection Agency) recommends that you do not use water taken from the hot tap for cooking or drinking.

**SAVE FOR STOCK:**
Cooked beef bones and beef trimmings, onion trimmings, carrot trimmings, beet ends left after grating (they will dye the stock red and lend a sweet flavor, which works well in tomato-based soups but not so well in green soups), tough parsnip cores, celery ends, and dill stems. Discard cabbage cores as their flavor is too strong for stock.

# Chapter 8
# CHOWDERS

Chunky, Creamy
Pennsylvania Dutch Chowder
gets its smoky flavor from
double-smoked bacon.

CHOWDER IN ITS INNUMERABLE VERSIONS provokes both strong feelings and contradictory claims, though most food historians agree that it derives from the French *chaudière*, a large iron cauldron in which sailors from Brittany on France's Atlantic Coast tossed their catch to make a communal stew on board ship. Another possible source is the old English term *jowter* for a vendor of fish. It was perhaps a New World marriage of the French fisherman's stew and the English layered fish pie with salt pork. This shipboard stew traveled across the Atlantic first to Canada's Maritime Provinces and then down east into New England.

It didn't take long for chowder to become a staple dish in New England and the Canadian Maritimes, with their large populations of sailors. Early chowders were quite thick with crumbled, dense ship's biscuits, also known as common crackers or hardtack, which made them easier to eat on board. Regional variations began to develop in the early nineteenth century. Maine became known for lobster chowder and Boston for creamy clam chowder, though cod and haddock chowder were far more common. On Nantucket Island, home to seafaring whalers, the simplest of chowders included only fish or clams, salt pork, onions, salt, and pepper, thickened with flour with water for the liquid. Eventually, milk and cream replaced the water, especially in regions rich with dairy products, and butter was added for enrichment. Meatier bacon began to replace heavily salted salt pork toward the end of the nineteenth century.

By the 1830s, Rhode Island cooks were adding newfangled tomatoes to their chowder, a desecration that was abhorred by northern New England cooks. This tomato-based soup became known as Manhattan clam chowder, perhaps because harvesting clams and growing tomatoes were economically important on Long Island and were often shipped to Manhattan. Another possibility is that Neapolitan immigrants adapted their traditional tomato and clam stew to American ingredients and palates. As early as 1751, a chowder recipe included pepper, salt, parsley, marjoram, savory, and thyme. Spices such as allspice, cloves, red pepper, curry powder, and Worcestershire sauce began showing up in more sophisticated versions of this simple fisherman's stew.

In this chapter, we prepare Alaska Wild Salmon Chowder with Bacon, Leeks, and Dill (page 126) using firm, deep red wild Alaska sockeye salmon rather than Atlantic salmon, which is now only available farm raised. The Scallop and White Corn Chowder with Roasted Poblano Chiles (page 124) is a nontraditional but hearty vegetarian soup best when sweet corn is in season. The New England–Style Clam Chowder (page 128) includes parsnips, which were far more popular in the past than today, along with fragrant celery root. The Pennsylvania Dutch Bacon, Corn, and Potato Chowder (page 130) includes corn and bell peppers in a creamy broth. The New England-Style Clam Chowder (page 128) developed on the Atlantic Islands of Nantucket and Martha's Vineyard.

# SCALLOP AND WHITE CORN CHOWDER WITH ROASTED POBLANO CHILES

THIS NONTRADITIONAL CHOWDER combines sweet sea scallops with tender white corn kernels and a spicy edge of mildly hot, smoky fire-roasted poblano chiles, which are all at their best in early autumn. For a heartier soup, add 1 pound (455 g) yellow potatoes, peeled and diced, after adding the flour and cook for about 10 minutes before adding the corn and diced poblanos. Poblanos, known as Ancho chiles when smoke-dried (and called Pasilla in California), come from Puebla, known for its sophisticated cuisine and the skill of its chefs. A large chile shaped like a long pointed heart, the poblano is deep green, moderately hot, and meaty in texture. This soup doesn't freeze well.

**Makes about 3 quarts (3 L), serves 8 to 10**

### INGREDIENTS

- 2 poblano chiles
- 6 ears white corn
- 1½ pounds (680 g) sea scallops (untreated)
- 1 sweet onion, diced
- ¼ cup (56 g) unsalted butter
- ¼ cup (32 g) all-purpose flour
- 2 quarts (2 L) Vegetable, Fish, or Shrimp Stock (page 14, 12, or 11), simmering
- 3 large sprigs thyme, tied in string with 2 bay leaves
- 1 cup (235 ml) heavy cream (substitute light cream or half and half if desired)
- Kosher salt and freshly ground black pepper to taste

## SOUPMAKER'S TIP

❋ Small, hard, striated "catch" muscles may be attached to the side of the scallops. Grab the muscle firmly, coaxing it away from the scallop with a paring knife, and then pull it off the scallop. Tough texture equals potent flavor, so don't throw these away. Use them to flavor the soup before straining. Alternatively, wrap and freeze them for use in a future seafood-based stock.

**1.** Char the poblanos either over an open gas flame or directly on an electric stove coil or ceramic top, turning the chiles as they blacken. The chiles will produce a lot of smoke.

**2.** Cool the chiles, then rub off the skins. Have a bowl of cold water ready. Dip your hands into the water to rinse the charred chile skin pieces off.

**3.** Pull off and discard the stem and inner seeds. Rinse briefly to remove the remainder.

**4.** Place a cleaned poblano so that it lies flat. Slice into strips, then cut the strips into dice.

**5.** Cut the corn kernels off the cobs (see Appendix, page 145) and reserve.

**6.** Trim off any small, hard "catch" muscles (see "Soupmaker's Tips," page 53) on the sides of the scallops as well as any intestinal veins, which run like a belt on the outside of the scallops, if present. Cut the scallops into small, bite-size bits and reserve, chilled.

**7.** In a large soup pot, cook the onions in the butter until transparent but not browned. Stir in the flour. Cook for 3 to 4 minutes to cook out the raw taste.

**8.** Pour in the simmering stock (here tomato-based Shrimp Stock) and whisk to combine well so the soup thickens evenly. Add the thyme and bay leaves.

**9.** Pour in the cream while stirring to incorporate it evenly.

**10.** Add the corn kernels and then add the diced roasted chiles. Bring to a boil, stirring until the broth is smooth, about 5 minutes.

**11.** At the last minute, add the scallops. Cook only long enough for the scallops to get firm and opaque, about 2 minutes, stirring so they cook evenly. Season the chowder with salt and pepper and serve immediately.

**SAVE FOR STOCK:**
Corncobs, onion trimmings, thyme stems, scallop "catch" muscles

# ALASKA WILD SALMON CHOWDER WITH BACON, LEEKS, AND DILL

WITH ALL THE TECHNOLOGICAL advances that have been made in freezing techniques, often the "freshest" fish will be found frozen. Here we use wild Alaska sockeye salmon with its intense persimmon-red color and dense, lean flesh that has been filleted and frozen. When working with frozen fish, cook when the fish is not yet completely defrosted so that all the juices haven't leaked out. Farmed Atlantic salmon is an acceptable, but not ideal, substitute. Look for frozen wild sockeye salmon in summer and early fall at warehouse club stores and other market.

**Makes about 5 quarts (5 L), serves 12 to 16**

### INGREDIENTS

- ½ pound (225 g) sliced bacon, chilled
- 2 pounds (907 g) wild salmon fillet, pin bones removed
- 1 bunch leeks, trimmed, quartered lengthwise, sliced, washed, scooped from the water, and drained (see Appendix, page 153)
- 6 sprigs thyme, tied with kitchen string
- 1 bay leaf
- Large pinch dried hot red pepper flakes
- 6 tablespoons (47 g) all-purpose flour
- 1 quart (1 L) liquid (canned salmon juices combined with water) or you may use Fish Stock or Vegetable Stock, page 12 or 14)
- 1 quart (1 L) whole milk
- 2 cups (475 ml) light or heavy cream
- 1 pound (455 g) gold potatoes, cut into ¾-inch (1.5 cm) dice (unpeeled if skins are thin, peeled if skins are thick)
- 1 small celery root, pared and diced (see Appendix, page 152)
- Sea salt and freshly ground black pepper
- ¼ cup (13 g) chopped dill, plus extra for garnish
- Grated zest of 2 lemons

**Diced leek, onion, and gold potato ready for a pot of chowder**

1. Cut sliced bacon into ¼-inch (6 mm) strips and crosswise into ¼-inch (6 mm) dice. This is easier if the bacon is well-chilled or partially frozen.

2. Cook bacon in a large heavy-bottomed soup pot over moderate heat, stirring occasionally, until crisp, about 8 minutes. Transfer with a slotted spoon to paper towels to drain.

3. Meanwhile, remove the skin from the fish fillets, which may be in individual portions, as here, or a part or a whole side of salmon. Lay the fillet down on the counter. Grasping the back of the fillet with your nondominant hand, use a sharp boning or special flexible fish filleting knife to slice between the skin and the flesh.

4. Grasp the tab you've just created with your nondominant hand. While pulling back on the skin tab, begin cutting with the knife from the end of the tab to the end of the fillet using a sawing motion.

5. Keep the knife angled down toward the skin rather than up and toward the flesh. Remove and discard the skin once it has been freed from the fillet. Cut the fish into ½- to ¾-inch (1 to 1.5 cm) cubes and reserve, refrigerated.

6. Pour off all but ¼ cup (60 ml) fat from the pot. Add leeks, thyme, bay leaf, and red pepper flakes. Cook over moderate heat, stirring occasionally, until tender, about 5 minutes.

7. Stir in the flour, which should absorb all the fat, and cook, stirring, 3 minutes to remove raw flour taste.

8. Add salmon juice mixture or stock, milk, and cream and bring just to a boil, stirring, so that the liquid thickens evenly from the flour.

9. Add potatoes and celery root and bring back to a boil. Reduce heat to moderately low and simmer about 10 minutes or until potatoes are almost tender.

10. Add the cooked bacon, salt and pepper to taste, dill, and lemon zest and cook, gently stirring occasionally.

11. Add the reserved salmon and cook until barely cooked through, avoiding overcooking, about 5 minutes. Discard bay leaf and thyme bundle before serving. Garnish with dill.

12. Salmon chowder, piping hot and ready to eat. Extra chowder may be cooled, transferred to smaller containers, and frozen up to 3 months.

# NEW ENGLAND-STYLE CLAM CHOWDER

IN 1751, THE *BOSTON EVENING POST* published an early recipe for chowder containing onions, salt pork, marjoram, savory, thyme, ship's biscuit, and fish, to which was added a bottle of red wine. Thickened from the crumbled common crackers, hardtack, or ship's biscuit, early chowders were more like stew than soup, best for onboard consumption in stormy weather. You may use packaged chopped clams, often available at the seafood counter, or small, fresh clams steamed open. New England-style clam chowder is enriched with cream and these days usually smoky bacon rather than salt pork.

**Makes about 1 gallon (4 L), serves 8 to 12**

### INGREDIENTS

- ½ pound (225 g) bacon, cut into small strips and then diced
- 1 large onion, diced
- 3 to 4 ribs celery, sliced
- ½ cup (63 g) all-purpose flour
- 2 quarts (2 L) milk, scalded
- 1 cup (235 ml) heavy cream
- 1 quart (1 L) bottled clam broth, juice from steamed clams, or Shrimp Stock (page 11)
- 2 large Idaho or gold potatoes, peeled and cut into small dice
- 2 dozen small clams (see "Preparing and Steaming Fresh Clams," opposite) or 1-pint (261 g) container chopped clams
- 2 tablespoons (8 g) chopped Italian parsley, plus extra for garnish
- 2 tablespoons (5 g) finely chopped thyme and/or marjoram
- 2 bay leaves
- ½ teaspoon ground allspice
- Black pepper and cayenne pepper
- Hot red pepper flakes (optional), for garnish

1

2

5

6

1. Sauté the bacon over low heat in a large soup pot until most of the fat is rendered.

2. Add the onion and celery and cook over medium heat until softened but not browned.

3. Stir in the flour and cook 3 to 4 minutes to get rid of the raw flour taste.

4. Pour in the hot milk and cream and clam broth and bring to a boil, stirring, until the broth thickens evenly.

5. Add the potatoes, and bring back to a boil. Simmer about 10 minutes or until the potatoes are tender.

6. Add the clams, chopped herbs, bay leaves, and allspice. Bring back to a boil, season to taste with pepper and cayenne.

7. Pour into serving bowls, sprinkle with a little hot red pepper flakes and chopped parsley if desired, and serve.

## Preparing and Steaming Fresh Clams

Scrub the clams using an abrasive scouring pad, then soak for 30 minutes in cold, salted water with 2 tablespoons (18 g) of cornmeal added to help purge them. Remove clams from water, taking care to leave any sand undisturbed, and discard water.

2

3

Place the clams into a large pot and add 1 cup (235 ml) water, white wine, or dry white vermouth. Cover and turn the heat to high.

1. Steam the clams just until their shells fully open, removing each clam from the pot as its shell opens and shaking the pot so the clams steam open evenly. Discard any clams that were not closed or which do not open after steaming for 5 to 10 minutes.

2. Set up two bowls. Pluck the clams from their shells, placing the meats in one bowl and the shells in another. Discard the shells.

3. Strain the clam broth through a dampened paper towel laid into a sieve to remove any sand, or leave behind the last ½ cup (120 ml) or so of broth, which will contain most of any remaining sand.

# PENNSYLVANIA DUTCH BACON, CORN, AND POTATO CHOWDER

THIS THICK AND CREAMY soup is packed full of chunky potato, peppers, corn, and bacon, and is filling enough to serve at a Pennsylvania Dutch barn raising. If you like, use double-smoked bacon, found at Pennsylvania Dutch or German butcher shops, for a more intensely smoky flavor. Either cooked or raw corn will work here, but the soup will taste best if made with fresh young corn cut from the cob. It is made with Vegetable or Chicken Stock, milk, and cream. Because it contains both potatoes and cream, this soup does not freeze well. It will keep up to 5 days refrigerated.

**Makes about 1 gallon (4 L), serves 8 to 12**

### INGREDIENTS

- ½ pound (225 g) well-smoked country-style bacon strips, cut into ½-inch (1 cm) slices and then diced
- 1 large onion, diced
- 3 ribs celery, thinly sliced
- 1 red bell pepper, diced
- 1 green pepper, diced
- ¼ cup (32 g) all-purpose flour
- 1 quart (1 L) Vegetable or Chicken Stock (page 14 or 9)
- 2 pounds (907 g) gold potatoes, diced into ½-inch (1 cm) cubes
- 6 ears corn, kernels cut off (see Appendix, page 145)
- 2 quarts (2 L) milk, scalded
- 1 cup (235 ml) heavy cream
- Kosher salt and freshly ground black pepper
- ½ bunch chives, thinly sliced (optional), for garnish

Sauté bacon over low heat in a large soup pot until most of the fat is rendered.

**1.** Add the onion, celery, red and green pepper, and simmer until tender but not browned.

Stir in the flour and cook for 3 to 4 minutes to cook out the raw taste.

**2.** Add the Vegetable Stock and potatoes and cook all together until the potatoes are soft, about 10 minutes, stirring to combine well so the soup thickens evenly without developing lumps.

**3.** Bring the soup back to a boil, stirring to make sure it doesn't stick and burn.

**4.** Add the corn, stirring to combine. Cook about 5 minutes or until the corn is cooked through.

**5.** Pour in the hot milk and cream, stir to combine, and season to taste with salt and pepper.

**6.** Serve garnished with thinly sliced chives, if desired, and serve.

# SOUPMAKER'S TIPS

❋ You may use leftover cooked corn on the cob here. If using raw corn kernels, add to the pot during the last 5 minutes of cooking the potatoes. If using cooked corn, add the corn kernels when the potatoes are soft.

**SAVE FOR STOCK:**
Onion and celery trimmings, green and red pepper cores and stem sections, potato trimmings, and corncobs.

# Chapter 9
# CHILLED SOUPS

Bright and lively sweet green pea soup is garnished with snow pea julienne and served in small shooter glasses.

THE REFRESHING SOUPS in this chapter will help keep you cool inside and out in hot weather and most are made without stock. They include two different gazpachos, one based on tomato and one based on green grapes. These are essentially salad soups from the Spanish and Arabic traditions, tart with a few drops of vinegar and enriched with the fruity green olive Spain exports in great quantities.

You may not be familiar with cold fruit soups such as the simmered, strained and Chilled Apricot Soup with Star Anise (page 134). These soups come from the eastern and northern European tradition of serving cold, clear fruit soup in summer made from fresh stone fruits such as apricots, plums, and cherries, or berries such as red currants, raspberries, and bilberries (alternatively, it is made in winter from dried fruits). Apples, gooseberries, rose hips, and rhubarb also show up in fruit soup. The soup may be thin and delicate or thickened and substantial or even served molded like kisel, not far from the classic French *consommé madrilène*, a jellied clear tomato soup now out of fashion.

*Kisel* is a Slavic fruit soup, popular as a dessert, made from sweetened fruit juice with red wine, fresh or dried fruits, thickened with starch. It is similar to Danish *rodegrod* and German *rote grütze*. Kisel can be served either hot or cold, and it is served with sweetened quark—a very tart fresh cheese—or semolina pudding. It may top pancakes or ice cream. In Russia, kisel is usually thinner and served as a drink. *Schav* is another Russian summer cold soup made from sour

sorrel leaves and *smetana*—sour cream. Tartness from fruits, herbs, and berries, and tangy fresh dairy products such as sour cream, buttermilk, and yogurt are common denominators of traditional chilled northern summer soups. Lemon and vinegar play the same refreshing role in Spanish gazpacho.

The Chilled Melon, Yogurt, and Ginger Soup (page 136) is a purée of ripe summer melon accented by tart yogurt and grated fresh ginger root, which should be served within a few days as the uncooked melon purée won't keep long. The brightly colored Chilled Green Pea and Snow Pea Soup with Mint (page 142) is flavored with cooling mint and easy to make using frozen baby peas.

With all chilled soups, season generously, as cold dulls flavors, and serve them quite cold in chilled bowls if possible. Garnish with a dollop of tangy sour cream or yogurt if desired. Keep in mind that soups will thicken substantially when chilled so thicken lightly. It's your choice whether to serve fruit soup as a first course or dessert.

# CHILLED APRICOT SOUP WITH STAR ANISE

COLD STONE FRUIT SOUPS, a summertime favorite in the former Austro-Hungarian Empire, are typically made from apricots, prune plums, or sour cherries. The clear, wine-enhanced, slightly thickened soup is usually finished with a generous dollop of sour cream. Here we simmer the apricots in a cinnamon stick, star anise, and bay leaf-infused syrup for a spiced sweet-tart soup that may be served as either a first course, especially for lunch or brunch, or for dessert accompanied by shortbread cookies often including ground hazelnuts.

**Makes about 3 quarts, 3 L, serves 6 to 9**

### INGREDIENTS

- 3 pounds (1.4 k) fresh apricots, or 1 pound dried apricots, preferably Blenheim
- ¾ cup (175 ml) sugar
- ¾ cup (175 ml) honey
- 1 stick cinnamon
- 4 whole star anise pods
- 2 bay leaves
- ½ teaspoon salt
- ½ teaspoon ground black pepper
- ¼ (60 ml) cup cornstarch
- ½ (120 ml) cup water or orange juice
- ¾ cup (175 ml) dry red wine, chilled
- 1 cup (235 ml) sour cream
- 6 to 8 star anise pods or mint sprigs (for garnish)

1  2  3  4  5

**1.** If using fresh apricots, half and pit them. Set aside.

**2.** If using dried apricots, cover with cold water and soak several hours or overnight, refrigerated, until softened.

**3.** In a large soup pot, combine 2 quarts (2 L) water, sugar, honey, cinnamon, star anise, bay leaves, salt, and black pepper. Bring to a boil and simmer 30 minutes to infuse the liquid with the spice flavors.

**4.** Add the apricots and any soaking liquid and bring back to a boil, skimming off the foam impurities. Reduce the heat and simmer until the apricots are quite soft, about 30 minutes. Fish out the cinnamon stick, 4 star anise pods (count them), and 2 bay leaves.

**5.** Meanwhile, mix the cornstarch with ½ cup (120 ml) water (or orange juice) to make a slurry (thin paste).

**6.** Beat cornstarch slurry into the hot soup while stirring constantly. Continuing to stir, bring the soup back to a boil and then remove from heat.

**7.** Ladle the hot soup into a blender jar, cover tightly, and blend, always starting on the lowest speed to prevent hot soup from splattering. Blend and then strain the soup through a food mill. For a finer texture, strain again through a fine sieve, discarding any solids.

**8.** Cool, add the red wine, and then chill soup in the refrigerator.

**9.** Top each serving with a spoonful of sour cream and a star anise pod or a sprig of fresh mint.

6  7

## SOUPMAKER'S TIPS

✣ Form the sour cream into a quenelle or egg shape using either one or two soupspoons turned around in the sour cream several times and then dropped into the soup.

**Choosing dried apricots:** The most common dried apricots in the market come from Turkey; they are dried in whole form with their pits removed. They are light yellow-orange with somewhat tough wrinkly skin. California apricots are pitted and halved before drying and are deeply colored with velvety skin and dense, jammy but melting texture. Soft, luscious Blenheim apricots are a highly prized variety similar to the French Royal apricot, originally grown at England's Blenheim Castle and planted in California in the 1880s. Note that if dried apricots have sat on the shelf too long, they may be hard, dark, and leathery, so buy them from a place that turns them over quickly, such as a natural foods market.

# CHILLED MELON, YOGURT, AND GINGER SOUP

HERE IS AN EASY WAY to make refreshing, tangy chilled soup for a hot summer's day, though you will need a blender, a food processor, or even a vegetable juicer such as an Acme or Champion. Plan on making the soup when local juicy, sweet cantaloupes or other orange-fleshed melons, such as Tuscan, or orange-fleshed honeydew or muskmelons, are in season. Thick Greek yogurt, which is drained of its excess whey, adds a concentrated flavor. You may substitute plain yogurt for a slightly thinner soup. Cooling mint makes the soup even more refreshing.

**Makes about 1 gallon (4 L), 8 to 12 servings**

### INGREDIENTS

- 3 to 4 ripe cantaloupes, about 6 pounds (2.7 kg)
- 2 cups (475 ml) orange juice
- 1 cup (230 g) Greek yogurt
- 2 tablespoons (16 g) grated ginger
- ½ cup (170 g) honey
- ¼ cup (23 g) mint leaves, preferably spearmint
- ½ cup (120 ml) lime juice
- 1 teaspoon (6 g) kosher salt
- Grated zest of 1 lime
- 1 jalapeno, seeded and minced
- 2 to 3 kiwi, cut into small cubes, for garnish
- Small wedge watermelon, red and/or yellow, cut into small cubes, for garnish
- Mint sprigs, for garnish

Ingredients for melon soup. Cantaloupe is best because of its appealing orange color, but other juicy yellow or orange melons, such as Canary or Crenshaw, will also work. A yellow watermelon would make a lovely soup, but because it is so sweet, eliminate most of the honey.

1. Prepare the melon (after washing well, see "Soupmaker's Tips: Cantaloupes and Salmonella") by laying it on its side and cutting off a slice from the top and bottom ends. This creates a stable flat surface for further cutting.

2. Preferably using a flexible-bladed knife (here a boning knife), cut away the outer skin and greenish layer just below the surface in strips about 1½-inches (3.5 cm) wide.

3. Curve the knife to follow the shape of the melon. Trim away any remaining bits of green or skin.

4. Place the peeled melon with its flat side down on the work surface and then cut in half "through the poles."

5. Open up the melon.

6. Use a large soup spoon to scrape out the inner seed portion. If desired, to extract as much juice as possible, transfer the seed portion to a sieve placed over a bowl and press to release any juices. Discard the remainder.

Cut the melon into rough cubes before proceeding with the recipe.

7. Combine the melon, orange juice, yogurt, ginger, honey, mint, lime juice, and salt in a blender jar.

8. Blend the soup ingredients until smooth. Or, place the ingredients in the bowl of a food processor and process—noting that a blender will yield the smoothest soup.

9. Work in two or three batches if necessary. If doing so, combine all batches in a large bowl and whisk to mix evenly.

10. Transfer the liquid to a large bowl and whisk in the lime zest and jalapeno. Chill the soup at least 1 hour before serving.

11. Pour into serving bowls, chilled if you prefer the soup extra cold, and garnish with diced kiwi and watermelon and/or a sprig of mint.

11

# SOUPMAKER'S TIPS

❈ Serve this chilled soup in small glass or ceramic shooter glasses for a light and elegant make-ahead starter. This soup does not freeze well.

**Cantaloupes and Salmonella:** Cantaloupe melons have been linked to at least two salmonella outbreaks. To prevent any possible contamination, use a produce scrub brush, (a brush with deep bristles), to scrub the outside of the cantaloupes thoroughly before cutting them open. Afterward, wash your hands, countertops, and any kitchen tools.

# GOLDEN TOMATO GAZPACHO WITH SMOKED PAPRIKA

GAZPACHO COMES FROM SPAIN and is the southern region of Andalusia's best-known dish. Its origins date back to the 700-year period in which Spain was part of the Islamic world. Before Columbus brought tomatoes and peppers to the Old World, gazpacho was a simple mash of olive oil, bread, and garlic with vinegar. Modern recipes for gazpacho in the Andalusian style, served as refreshing cold soup with finely chopped garnishes, include the New World tomato—here low-acid golden tomatoes—with golden saffron added for color and distinct, slightly acrid flavor. In a well-made gazpacho, no one ingredient stands out and the whole is greater than the sum of its parts.

### Makes about 1 gallon (4 L), serves 8 to 12

### INGREDIENTS

- 1 cup Toasted Garlic Croutons (recipe follows)
- 3 tablespoons (45 ml) sherry vinegar
- 1 large pinch saffron threads (optional)
- 1 quart (1 L) Vegetable Stock (page 14), divided
- 3 pounds (1.4 kg) ripe golden tomatoes, cored and cut into large chunks
- 2 yellow bell peppers, seeded and cut into large chunks
- 3 medium cloves garlic
- 2 pounds (907 g) cucumbers, peeled and cut into large chunks
- ½ medium red onion, cut into large chunks
- 1 tablespoon (19 g) kosher salt
- 1½ teaspoons (4 g) pimentón dulce (Spanish sweet smoked paprika), substitute paprika
- ½ teaspoon freshly ground pepper
- ½ cup (120 ml) extra-virgin olive oil, plus extra for garnish
- Finely diced red and yellow pepper, tomato, red onion, cucumber, thinly sliced chives, and more Toasted Garlic Croutons, for garnish

Ingredients for Golden Tomato Gazpacho with Smoked Paprika—a blender is essential!

1

2

4 5

6 8

**1.** Soak the croutons in the vinegar mixed with about ½ cup (120 ml) water until soft, about 15 minutes.

Soak the saffron, if using, in about ½ cup (120 ml) of the Vegetable Stock until golden in color, about 15 minutes.

**2.** Working in several batches, transfer the soaked croutons, yellow tomatoes, peppers, garlic, cucumbers, onion, salt, pimentón, and pepper in the jar of a blender, and pour in the olive oil.

**3.** Add enough Vegetable Stock to cover the vegetables by about 1 inch (2.5 cm). Blend to a smooth purée. Repeat process for the next batch, pouring in more Vegetable Stock to cover.

**4.** While optional, straining through a food mill fitted with a medium-holed plate will result in a smooth-textured soup.

**5.** The food mill will remove any seeds and remaining bits of skin. Correct seasoning if necessary. Chill soup thoroughly before serving.

**6.** Drizzle a trace of olive oil onto each serving.

**7.** Garnish each serving with a spoonful of combined diced or julienned pepper, tomato, onion, and cucumber along with a spoonful of croutons. Or, pass around small bowls of the garnishes for each guest to garnish their own soup to taste.

**8.** If desired, sprinkle each portion with thinly sliced chives and saffron just before serving. Store soup covered and refrigerated up to 4 days. (This soup does not freeze successfully.)

# TOASTED GARLIC CROUTONS

**Makes about 4 cups (112 g)**

- 1 loaf (1 to 1½ pounds, or 455 to 680 g) stale hearty French or Italian bread, crusts removed if desired
- ¾ cup (175 ml) extra-virgin olive oil
- 3 large cloves garlic, crushed

Preheat the oven to 350°F (180°C, or gas mark 4). Cut bread into ½-inch (1 cm) cubes and place in a large bowl. Add the oil and garlic and toss well to combine. Spread the bread cubes out in a single layer on a baking pan. Bake 20 minutes, stirring once, or until the bread cubes are golden brown. Cool to room temperature before storing in an airtight container for up to 1 week.

# GREEN GAZPACHO WITH GARLIC, GRAPES, AND ALMONDS

ROMAN LEGIONS would each carry their essential foods of bread, garlic, salt, olive oil, and vinegar on their lengthy treks along the vast road system of the Empire, each soldier making his own mixture to taste. These foods formed the basis of gazpacho, which was also influenced by the Arabs who brought ingredients such as saffron, almonds, coriander, and pine nuts into the cuisine of the Iberian Peninsula. This green gazpacho is based on those same ingredients: bread, garlic, salt, olive oil, and vinegar—but may include almonds (as here); pine nuts; green melon; green apple; green grapes; herbs such as coriander, mint, and parsley; and salad greens such as lettuce, endive, and spinach.

**Makes about 3 quarts (3 L)**

### INGREDIENTS

- 2 cucumbers, peeled, seeded, and coarsely chopped
- 3 ounces (about 2 cups, or 85 g) baby spinach
- 1 pound (455 g) seedless green grapes, picked off their stems
- 1 green or yellow bell pepper, coarsely chopped
- 1 bunch green onions, thinly sliced
- 3 ounces (about 2 cups, or 85 g) crumbled crusty white bread, crusts removed and discarded
- 1 quart (1 L) water, divided
- ½ pound (225 g) blanched almonds
- 2 tablespoons (30 ml) Sherry wine vinegar
- ¼ cup (60 ml) extra-virgin olive oil, plus extra for garnish
- 2 garlic cloves, minced
- 2 tablespoons (8 g) coarsely chopped fresh cilantro
- Salt and freshly ground black pepper
- Thinly sliced chives or chopped cilantro, for garnish

1. Combine cucumbers, spinach, grapes, bell pepper, and green onions in a large bowl.

2. Place the bread in a bowl and cover with about 1 cup (235 ml) of the water.

3. Let the bread soak until soft and soggy, about 5 minutes. Add the soaked bread and the soaking liquid to the bowl of mixed vegetables and fruit.

4. Add the almonds to the bowl.

5. Add the vinegar, olive oil, garlic, and cilantro to the bowl and toss with your clean and/or gloved hands to combine well.

6. Working in two to three batches, fill the jar of a blender about three-quarters of the way up. (Because the soup isn't hot, you may fill the blender jar without concern for splattering hot soup.) Pour in enough of the water to cover the mixture.

7. Purée until smooth, adding more of the remaining water if needed to thin the mixture enough so it will blend.

Transfer gazpacho to a large bowl and season with salt and pepper to taste. Note that cold soups should be seasoned more generously than hot soups as cold dulls the flavor. Cover and refrigerate at least 2 hours.

8. Ladle the soup into serving bowls and serve chilled.

9. Garnish with a drizzle of extra-virgin olive oil and a sprinkle of chives or a small sprig of cilantro.

# CHILLED GREEN PEA AND SNOW PEA SOUP WITH MINT

THIS BRILLIANT GREEN SOUP is smooth and silky in texture with a sprightly fresh note of mint. It is quite easy to make using frozen *petit pois*, or baby peas. Larger full-grown peas will be starchier and heavier. It is not necessary to cook the peas, simply rinse the frozen peas under cold water to remove any frost, which absorbs odors, blend and strain. Here we garnish the soup with blanched (par-cooked) snow peas cut into julienne strips and a tiny dollop of sour cream and serve it in small "shooter" glasses—perfect for a spring or summer brunch, lunch, or buffet. Made with Vegetable Stock, this is a vegetarian soup. Served without the sour cream garnish, it is also vegan.

**Makes 1 gallon (4 L), serves 8 to 12**

### INGREDIENTS

- 3 quarts (3 L) cold Vegetable Stock (page 14)
- ½ cup (45 g), or about 1 bunch, fresh mint, coarsely chopped
- 3 pounds (1.4 kg) frozen baby green peas, thawed under cold running water
- ½ cup (30 g), or about 1 bunch, Italian parsley leaves, coarsely chopped
- 2 bunches scallions, sliced or 1 sweet onion, sliced`
- ½ cup (120 ml) extra-virgin olive oil
- 2 tablespoons (26 g) sugar
- About ½ teaspoon freshly grated nutmeg
- Salt, ground nutmeg, and freshly ground black pepper
- ¼ pound (115 g) snow peas, (see "Preparing Snowpeas," page 143)
- 1 cup (230 g) sour cream, crème fraiche, or plain yogurt

## Preparing Snow Peas

Snow peas are quick-cooking and are sweet with a delicate crunch, but they benefit from careful preparation: removing their tough stem ends, the strings along their sides, and even the tiny white string often found on their blossom ends.

**1.** In a large bowl, mix the Vegetable Stock with the mint leaves, peas, parsley, scallions, oil, and sugar.

**2.** Using a Microplane or a nutmeg grater, grate the nutmeg into the soup.

**3.** Using a hand-held or traditional blender, purée the soup until quite smooth. If desired, strain through a sieve or food mill and then transfer back to the bowl. Season to taste with salt, ground nutmeg, and pepper.

Meanwhile, bring a small pot of salted water to a boil. Add the snow peas and cook briefly, 1 to 2 minutes, or until bright green. Drain and rinse under cold water to set the color. Cut into julienne (see Appendix, page 146) and reserve for garnish.

**4.** Serve the soup garnished with sour cream and the snow pea julienne. Store refrigerated up to 4 days or freeze if desired.

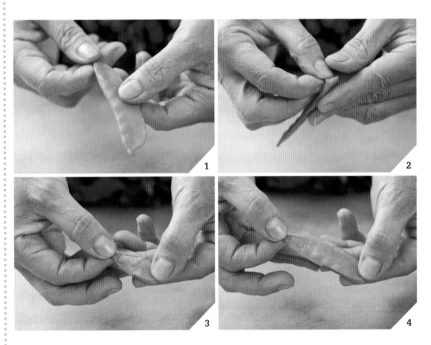

**1.** Grasp a snow pea in your hand with the pointier, harder stem end facing your dominant hand.

**2.** Pull on the end of the snow pea, breaking it backward.

**3.** Grasping the snow pea just past the broken edge with your non-dominant hand, pull back on the end toward your body.

**4.** Continue pulling to remove the strings on either side of the snow pea. Pull off the tiny white string on the bottom end of the snow pea.

# Appendix of Additional TECHNIQUES

## How to Chill Soup

One of the challenges of making soup and stock is that it is important to cool and then chill it quickly, especially in hot, humid weather when foods tend to spoil more readily. Follow the instructions here to get that soup or stock cooled quickly and safely.

**1. COOL:**

In cold weather, divide the stock into smaller containers and allow the stock to cool to warm room temperature, and then chill in the refrigerator. In hot weather, place the strained stock into a sink full of ice and water, or place a freezer gel pack inside a heavy-duty plastic bag into the stock to cool it quickly. Alternatively, use a submersible ice wand that can be filled with a mixture of ice cubes and water to stir through the soup and chill it quickly.

**2. CHILL:**

Transfer stock to storage containers or metal bowls and chill overnight. The next day, remove and discard any solidified fat from the top. Note that stock placed in a metal container or pot, preferably stainless steel, will cool more quickly than if it is placed in plastic or other less-conductive container. Do not place hot stock or soup directly in the refrigerator because it will warm up everything else in there, cutting down on shelf life and decreasing food safety. Freeze stock if desired. Always defrost in the refrigerator or in a container with cold water running over it.

**3. DEFAT:**

Once the stock has chilled, you may remove any layer of fat that will have risen to the top (not present in vegetable stocks). The fat forms a protective layer against bacteria while the stock is in the refrigerator. If you plan to freeze the stock, however, remove and discard the fat, and then pour the stock into a jar or plastic freezer container. Leave about 1 inch (2.5 cm) of headspace at the top of the freezer container because liquids expand as they freeze.

**4. STORE:**

For best shelf life, cool soup stock quickly. You may then refrigerate it for 3 to 4 days. Hearty long-cooked bean soups will last longer than quickly cooked clear soups such as chicken soup. Soups based on seafood—chowders and Mediterranean-style fish soup or stews, for example—will keep their sweet flavor for only 2 to 3 days. You may boil the soup or stock again anytime during this period to add a few more days of shelf life. Always sniff a container of stock from the refrigerator before using to make sure it hasn't spoiled.

## SOUPMAKER'S TIP

If time is short, consider using frozen vegetables, which just as high in nutrients as fresh and can be a big timesaver for your soups. Try frozen sliced leeks, chopped spinach, sliced carrots, garden peas, artichokes, collards, sweet peas, and asparagus. Asian and Indian markets are good places to find more exotic frozen vegetables such as fava beans, grated coconut, mustard greens, and sweet potatoes. Rinse the vegetables under cold water to get rid of frost which holds odors and undesirable flavors.

## Cutting Kernels off the Cob

**1.** Place the cob in its husk on the work surface with the stem end across from your dominant hand. Feel around the base of the cob to find where the cob ends and the narrower stem begins. Using a heavy chef's knife, cut off the bottom of the cob about ½ inch (1 cm) above the end of the cob. The more woody and difficult the cob is to cut through, the tougher the corn. A cob that is relatively easy to cut through will have tender, juicy, sweet kernels.

**2.** Turn the cob so the top is facing your dominant hand and feel around to where the main, thick portion of the cob begins and slice it off. (The top end has a narrower cone-shaped end with tiny, undeveloped kernels.)

**3.** Pull off the husk and inner layer of silks. (If desired, you may use the green husks to wrap tamales or fish for steaming, infusing them with corn flavor.)

Rub off any remaining silks (there is one silk for every kernel) with your hands or a clean kitchen scrub pad. Some small bits will inevitably remain.

**4.** Stand the cob on its larger end. Using a sharp chef's knife, cut down through the kernels, but not too deep into the cob or the kernels will be woody. The kernels will tend to fly away, so work away from the edge of the work surface. Cut in a strip about one-fifth of the distance around the cob.

**5.** Turn the cob and continue cutting in strips until you have removed all the kernels. Younger, smaller cobs mean less yield but usually sweeter flavor.

**6.** To extract the most in sweet corn goodness, use a sharp chef's knife to scrape off the corn "milk" contained in the cob, working in strips.

**Depending on the size, one corncob will yield ½ to 1 cup (77 to 154 g) of kernels.**

## Straining Broth through a Paper Towel

For a clearer broth, strain the broth while it is still hot and thin in consistency through a dampened paper towel laid into a wire sieve, which has been placed over a bowl. Or, use a large paper coffee filter. Use the bowl of a ladle to swirl the broth against the sieve encouraging the broth to fall into the bowl below. If the broth contains a lot of small bits of debris, you may need to change the towel before adding more broth for a second round of straining.

## Julienne Slicing Snow Peas

Snow peas are usually served whole, but they make a beautiful garnish for soup when cut into the long, thin strips known by the French term, *julienne*. Just a few are needed. The term *julienne* dates back about 300 years in print when it appeared in a French cookbook, *Le Cuisinier Royal et Bourgeois*, in a recipe for the soup Potage Julienne, which included carrots, beets, leeks, celery, lettuce, sorrel, and chervil all cut into delicate julienne strips.

**1.** To julienne, line up several snow peas, either raw or lightly blanched (cooked in boiling, salted water 1 minute and then rinsed under cold water to set the color), with their fatter, seeded side facing the knife, preferably a sharp chef's knife. (The younger and flatter the snow peas, the easier it will be to cut them.)

**2.** Slice the snow peas lengthwise into thin, fairly even strips, keeping your fingers curled so you don't cut them with the knife.

## SOUPMAKER'S TIPS

### USING FRESH HERBS

Aromatic fresh herbs, such as the dill, tarragon, and Italian parsley shown here, make for the freshest tasting soups. Use them generously, adding sprigs of herbs while simmering the soup, and then removing and discarding the herb sprigs before serving the soup. Finish the soup by adding chopped herbs near the end of cooking or just before serving.

Figure on using three to four times as much of the chopped fresh herb as its dried equivalent. Dried herbs make an acceptable though less sprightly substitute, but note many herbs—especially cilantro, parsley, and basil—lose most of their delicate flavor when dried.

# Chopping Large Amounts of Fresh Herbs

Pick the herbs and chop the same day as you'll be using them (because they break down quickly once chopped), using this technique.

**1.** Pick the leaves from their stems and arrange in a compact pile. Begin chopping, keeping your nondominant hand on the forward portion of the upper blade for control and using a rocking motion to chop.

**2.** Continue chopping, rocking the knife up and down and pivoting on its point moving in a fan shape from one side to the other. When you reach the end of the pile, use the knife to toss the herbs back together into a compact pile.

**3.** The herbs are ready when you have chopped them fine enough so that visible lines start to form after each chop of the knife, as in this photo.

# SOUPMAKER'S TIPS

If you do chop the herbs a day ahead of time, roll up in a paper towel to absorb excess moisture, place in a plastic bag and refrigerate up to 2 days. Always sniff prechopped herbs to make sure they haven't developed an unpleasant odor, which indicates that they've spoiled.

**SAVE FOR STOCK:**
Reserve the stems of tender herbs for stock. Do not use woody, resinous herb stems from savory, rosemary, oregano, and sage, which will be overly strong and slightly bitter if cooked. (You may collect these woody stems and throw them on the grill or in the smoker.)

## Studding an Onion with Cloves

The clove is a dried, unopened flower bud, and it has a potent, sweetly fiery taste that is delicious in small quantities but unpleasantly medicinal in larger amounts. Here we stick whole cloves into a peeled onion, which will simmer in broth, imparting a delicate clove flavor.

**1.** Using a pointed bamboo or metal skewer, stick one hole for each clove into a whole, peeled onion.

**2.** Insert one whole clove into each hole, pushing the clove in firmly to secure.

## Picking Mint (and Other) Fresh Herb Leaves

Fresh herbs lend their sprightly aroma to many soups. This technique will work for most tender herbs including basil, tarragon, marjoram, parsley, and cilantro.

**1.** Grasp the stem about one-third of the way from the top in your nondominant hand. Using that hand, pull downward on the lower portion of the leaves, detaching them from the stem so that the bottom portion of the stem is bare.

**2.** Still grasping the stem, use your dominant hand to pull upward to remove the more tender upper leaves and top sprig from the stem.

# Making a Bouquet Garni

A *bouquet garni* is a small bundle of aromatic ingredients such as herbs, peppercorns, and orange zest strips. This bundle is tied with kitchen string; enclosed in a piece of cheesecloth or undyed muslin; placed in a tea strainer, a coffee filter, or a special small net bag; or in traditional French kitchens, wrapped in leek leaves. The bouquet garni is added to soups, stocks, sauces, and stews, where it infuses the food with its aromas and is removed before serving. Most commonly, a bouquet garni will include parsley, thyme, and bay leaf, but often it includes basil, rosemary, sage, savory, and tarragon as well.

- 6 to 8 sprigs flat-leaf parsley
- 2 bay leaves
- 2 to 3 sprigs basil
- 3 to 4 sprigs thyme, marjoram, or savory
- 2 strips orange zest (one-quarter of an orange), cut using a potato peeler with a minimum of bitter, white pith

**1.** Make a compact bundle of the herbs and orange zest strips.

**2.** Either tie securely with kitchen string or place in a piece of muslin and tie shut. This makes it easy to remove the bundle after cooking.

# Soaking Saffron Threads

Saffron is the orange-red threadlike dried stigmas once attached to the base of the autumn flowering crocus flower. Its pungent, earthy, bittersweet flavor and acrid, haylike aroma complement fish and shellfish especially well. Saffron is the world's most expensive spice by weight, but because it is so concentrated, a few threads can flavor and color an entire dish. When purchasing saffron, check the harvest date, which should be of the current year, or at the latest, the past year. Avoid powdered saffron, which is easier to adulterate. Saffron may be stored, tightly sealed, in the freezer for up to two years with little loss of flavor.

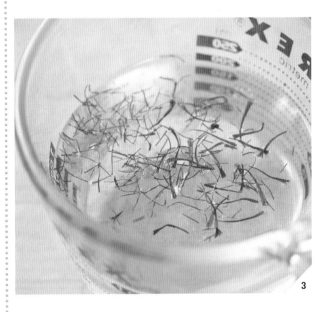

3

**1.** The best saffron includes only the pure deep red-orange stigmas; less expensive saffron bulks up with flavorless yellow stamens. Any "cheap saffron" is likely something else entirely.

**2.** Sprinkle the saffron threads into the wine.

**3.** Soak the saffron in the white wine about 15 minutes or until the liquid is deep gold in color.

# Dicing a Ripe Tomato

Dicing a ripe tomato without mashing it up is a challenge made easier by using a small serrated tomato knife.

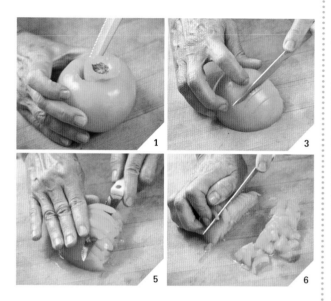

**1.** Cut away the tomato core in a cone shape. Save for stock if desired.

**2.** Cut the tomato in half "through the poles" rather than "through the equator."

**3.** Lay a half tomato flat side down on a cutting board and cut slices working from the blossom end toward the stem (core) end and leaving the slices attached at the blossom end.

**4.** Holding the tomato together with your nondominant hand, slice crosswise, at a slight downward angle to avoid cutting into your hand, three-quarters of the way through the tomato, leaving the slice attached at the blossom end.

**5.** Cut two more crosswise slices, keeping the knife at a slight downward angle and holding the tomato together with your other hand.

**6.** Now dice by slicing across the tomato and using your nondominant hand to hold the tomato together. Save the uncut tomato blossom ends for stock or sauce or chop by hand and add to the diced tomatoes.

# Cutting Basil Chiffonade

Basil darkens, or oxidizes, very easily if bruised, changing the flavor as well. To prevent this, always cut basil with a very sharp knife and slice, rather than chop, the leaves. Here we cut thin ribbons of basil by rolling the leaves up into a cigar-shape.

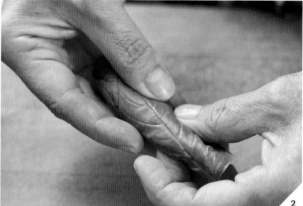

**1.** Start with the largest leaves, placing one on top of the other, vein side up, to form a fat stack of about 10 leaves. Place any smaller leaves on top.

**2.** Use the fingers of one hand to hold the leaves in place, and roll up the basil into a compact lengthwise tube with the seam underneath.

**3.** Using a sharp chef's knife, slice across the "cigar" to form thin ribbons of basil.

# Cooking and Mashing Lobster Roe

If you're lucky enough to find a mature female lobster that weighs at least 1½ pounds (680 g), you'll probably find it filled with dark, greenish-black roe (its unfertilized eggs), which is also known as lobster "coral" for the bright orange-red color it turns after cooking. Roe is considered a delicacy for its concentrated lobster flavor and gorgeous color. Smaller females will likely have underdeveloped roe, which will be light green and far less abundant. Here's how to cook lobster roe, which has very similar characteristics as cooking common hen eggs.

**1.** Place the roe sacs on a large piece of plastic film.

**2.** Roll up to make a "sausage," twisting the ends to make a compact bundle. Tie the ends securely shut. Place in a small pot of boiling water and cook until the roe turns completely red.

**3.** Unwrap the packet, place it in a sieve, and mash the roe against the sides of the sieve using a silicone spatula or a wooden pusher. Or, chop the roe into smaller chunks, place in the bowl of a food processor and process until finely ground.

**4.** Use as is or spread out on a parchment paper–lined baking pan. Bake at 300°F (150°C, or gas mark 2) for 10 minutes to dry out the roe for longer keeping (up to 1 week). The cooked roe also freezes well.

# How to Cut an Onion

Here is an efficient way to cut an onion that takes advantage of the onion's layered structure.

**1.** Place the onion on a work surface with its root end up. Grasping the side of the onion with your nondominant hand, cut straight through from the root to the stem. Pull off the outer layer of skin from one half of the onion using the stem end as a handle. Repeat with the second half. Trim off the stem of the onion.

**2.** Starting at the far side, cut thin even slices through one onion half, leaving the ends attached at the opposite root end. Hold the onion steady with the fingers of your other hand, curved to keep them away fromf the knife blade.

**3.** Place the sliced onion half flat side down, keeping it in place with the curved fingers of your other hand. Make a horizontal cut angled slightly toward the table to avoid your fingers and cutting through the onion but leaving the root end attached.

**4.** Make a second cut above the first also angling down.

**5.** Grasping the onion with your curved hand back at the root end, cut even crosswise slices forming small onion dice. Repeat with the other onion half. Save the onion skins, trimmings, and root ends for stock.

## Preparing Celery Root on the Branch

Celery root, or celeriac, is most commonly found minus its green tops, but the freshest, firmest celery root—minus the spongy center portion all too common in large, overgrown bare roots—is sold whole with tops. The greens are quite bitter and best used in small quantities only as a parsley-like herb.

**1.** Grasp the celery ribs in your nondominant hand. Using a sharp chef's knife, cut away the root from the ribs just below the ends of the ribs. Discard the dark green ribs.

**2.** Using a sharp chef's knife or a sturdy utility knife, pare away the darker outside layer of the celery root in strips, including the small rootlets on the bottom.

**3.** Save all the delicious trimmings for stock, transferring them to a bowl of cold water and swishing around vigorously to extract the dirt from the root ends. Once the trimmings are clean, drain and use for stock or transfer to a ziplock bag, and freeze up to 3 months.

**4.** Cut the pared celery root into ½-inch (1 cm) thick slices, and then cut the slices into even sticks about the same thickness. Line up the sticks and cut them crosswise into cubes of about the same thickness. Store in a bowl of cold water and refrigerate until ready to use, but use within 3 days.

## Slicing an Avocado

One of the most challenging but most rewarding vegetables is the avocado, preferably a rich buttery-fleshed Hass from California or Mexico, to which it is native. An avocado is ripe when you can easily pull out the stem end from the tip of the avocado. A Hass avocado is ripe when the skin turns waxy, rather than shiny, and is purplish-black, rather than green. Prepare the avocado as close as possible to the time that you'll be serving the soup as they quickly oxidize. Avoid using either underripe (hard and acrid in flavor) or overripe (mushy and bland in flavor) avocados.

**1.** Grasp the avocado in your nondominant hand with your fingers curled around one side. Use a sharp paring or boning knife to cut all around the circumference. The knife cut should meet at the tip where you began cutting to make a full circle around the avocado.

**2.** Grasp each half of the avocado in your hands and twist both halves in opposite directions. Pull apart the two avocado halves. The flesh should detach from the large center pit.

**3.** Cut the avocado halves in two to make four sections and pull out the pit. Use your knife to pull back on the skin. As seen here, the skin will pull away cleanly from a ripe avocado.

**4.** Slice each avocado quarter into three to five slices, and fan out the slices to separate them. Serve as a garnish for the soup.

# Tying Fresh Thyme into a Bundle

It's tedious work to pick off the small leaves of fresh thyme from the branch. Instead, when making soup, tie the sprigs together and simmer in the soup (or sauce). When ready to serve, just fish it out—most of the leaves will have fallen off into the soup but the tough branches will stay in the bouquet. Use the same technique with other fresh herbs such as tarragon, marjoram, or rosemary.

2

**1.** Cut off a length of kitchen string to about 8 inches (20 cm). Grab a small handful of thyme sprigs all lined up with their leaves at one end. Wrap the string tightly several times around the bundle.

**2.** Tie the string tightly into a secure knot and cut off any excess.

# Cutting and Cleaning Leeks

Leeks, which grow very slowly in the ground and consist of layer upon layer of leaves wrapped around each other, are notoriously difficult to clean because the dirt gets caught between the layers.

3    4

**1.** Cut off the white root end and save it for stock (use it in any kind of stock). Find where the white stalk begins to branch out into green leaves, and cut the leek at that point to form two fairly even sections.

**2.** Unwrap the tough, dark green outer leaves from the top section and discard them. (They are too strong in flavor and will darken any soup or stock to an unappealing color.) Reserve the remaining lighter green, tender sections.

**3.** Cut the bottom leek section into half lengthwise and then cut into quarters lengthwise. And then cut the reserved upper section into half lengthwise.

**4.** Line up all the leek pieces, grasping them together in a bunch with your nondominant hand. Slice crosswise to form small leek squares.

**5.** Transfer the cut leeks into a bowl of cold water and swish around vigorously to encourage any remaining dirt to drop to the bottom of the bowl. Scoop the washed leeks from the bowl using your hands or a wire skimmer and drain them in a colander.

# RESOURCES

## Suppliers

**WHOLE SPICE**
*Freshly ground, small-batch, hand-selected, roasted and blended spices*
www.wholespice.com

**FANTE'S KITCHENWARE**
*A large variety of kitchen tools including knives, strainers, china caps, heavy-duty, steel-lined copper pots which will last a lifetime*
www.fantes.com

**KALUSTYAN'S**
*Excellent line of spices, legumes, grains, nuts, spices, and ingredients, many from the Middle East and India*
www.kalustyans.com

## Websites & Online Articles

**CONVERT-TO.COM**
*Excellent resource for converting ingredients from weight to volume in U.S., Imperial, and metric measurements*
http://convert-to.com/conversion-of-ingredients-from-cooking-recipes

**THE FISH STEW WITH FIVE C'S**
*The fish stew of Livorno cacciucco: the fish stew with five c's and thirteen different types of seafood*
www.theflorentine.net/articles/article-view.asp?issuetocId=753

**BINNUR'S TURKISH COOKBOOK**
*Good on-line source for Turkish recipes, a cuisine rich in legumes, whole grains, vegetables, olive oil, and spices*
www.turkishcookbook.com

**GAZPACHO HISTORY**
*A fascinating subject with conflicting views on its origins—whether Roman or Arab or both. This will give insight as to where and how gazpacho got started.*
www.souphoopla.com/gazpacho-history.html

**THE FOOD TIMELINE**
*History notes and timeline for various soups including sources*
http://foodtimeline.org/foodsoups.html

**PRODUCE-RIPENING GUIDE FROM THE FORD'S PRODUCE COMPANY**
*Learn how to ripen fruits and vegetables, which produce gives off ethylene gas that helps ripen other produce and which items shouldn't be stored together*
www.fordsproduce.com/Fords-Produce-Fruit-Ripening-Guide.html

## Books

**50 Chowders: One Pot Meals—Clam, Corn & Beyond**
*Explore the world of chowders from New England lobster and Key West conch to parsnip and pheasant-cabbage in this small but well-researched book by famed New England chef, Jasper White* Scriber, New York, 2000

**Soup Through the Ages: A Culinary History with Period Recipes**
*Detailed history of soup including Biblical fare, Ancient Rome, Medieval Times, Renaissance Times, Colonial America, open-hearth cookery, American Indian soup cookery, by Victoria R. Rumble* McFarland & Company Publishers, North Carolina, 2009

**Chef's Book of Formulas, Yields, and Sizes**
*Resource for professional chefs and home cooks on pack sizes, counts, season, serving sizes, and calorie counts for a large variety of ingredients, by Arno Schmidt* John Wiley & Sons, New York 1996

**The Gold Cook Book**
*Classic culinary tome first published in 1947, by Louis De Gouy with many soup recipes* Chilton Company, Philadelphia, 1947 through 1960

# ACKNOWLEDGMENTS

My sincere thanks go to fellow members of Les Dames d'Escoffier Philadelphia Chapter who helped shop, prep, cook, and do the inevitable clean-up for our photo shoots. They include Adrienne Abramson, The Artful Chef, and Angie Brown, Soul Catering. I relied on Linda Gellman to help coordinate, prep, and critique the soups at each session. As a long-time catering production chef, Linda's excellent organization skills, unflagging encouragement, and salty sense of humor, helped make our photo shoots as much fun as they were productive. These three, as well as my dear friend and soup lover, Gail Morrison, lent me treasured soup bowls, ladles, and tureens from their personal collections that appear in many of the beautiful photos in this book.

I'd like to thank Ronit and Shuli Madrone, two Israeli-born spicemongers who carry an excellent selection of freshly ground small-batch, hand-selected and blended spices for their company, Whole Spice (www.wholespice.com). I used their Mediterranean dried spearmint, Turkish Urfa pepper, Syrian Aleppo pepper, Indian asafetida, Sri Lankan true cinnamon, Indian curry leaves, Mexican guajillo chiles, and Sichuan peppercorns, to name just a few. Their fragrant and boldly-flavored spices gave authentic flavor to these soups. If you're ever in Napa, California, stop in to their small, well-stocked spice stand at the Oxbow Market. They are especially knowledgeable about hard-to-find Turkish, Middle Eastern, and North African spices.

Once again, the Giovannucci family, owners of Philadelphia's historic and beloved culinary emporium, Fante's, (www.fantes.com), provided me with top-quality soup-making tools, pots and pans, and cutlery—the kind that you buy once in your life because they are so well made that they last for years and years. I particularly prize my Oxo food mill—all stainless steel with three removable plates—to make straining puréed soups a breeze.

My special thanks to Clare Pelino, of ProLiterary Agency, for connecting me and Quarry Books—quite a successful match as this is my fourth book with the company. I want to call out Tiffany Hill, my editor, who has been warm, encouraging, and always there to help me make this the best possible book. Also, project manager Betsy Gammons, who kept me in line so everything was done in a timely fashion, and art director David Martinell, who oversaw the design of this beautiful, highly informative book that is so easy for the reader to use. Copyeditor Kathy Dragolich has an enviable eye for detail ensuring that every recipe is correct. She's also a whiz at doing metric conversions, which allowed me more time to test the recipes and concentrate on writing.

We all ate a lot of soups this summer, including my neighbors at our annual block party to which I brought four pots of soup—all empty when I took them home. (Their favorites were the Rumanian Beet-Vegetable Borscht and the Scallop and White Corn Chowder.) With the *Soupmaker's Kitchen*, I hope that enthusiastic home cooks, chefs, and culinarians will be inspired to make their own stocks and deliciously seasonal soups from places as far flung as Vietnam, Rumania, Mexico, Italy, Alaska, Portugal, New Orleans, Turkey, Greece, Senegal, and Hungary in their own kitchens. Nothing is more welcoming than a big pot of soup simmering on the stove. Soup's on!

# ABOUT THE AUTHOR

**ALIZA GREEN** is an award-winning Philadelphia–based author, journalist, and influential chef whose books include *The Butcher's Apprentice* and *Making Artisan Pasta* (Quarry Books, 2012) selected by *Cooking Light Magazine* as one of their Top 100 Cookbooks of the Last 25 Years, *The Fishmonger's Apprentice* (Quarry Books, 2010), *Starting with Ingredients: Baking* (Running Press, 2008) and *Starting with Ingredients* (Running Press, 2006), four perennially popular field guides to food (Quirk, 2004–2007), *Beans: More than 200 Delicious, Wholesome Recipes from Around the World* (Running Press, 2004) and a successful collaboration with renowned chef Georges Perrier.

A former food columnist for the *Philadelphia Inquirer*, *Philadelphia Daily News*, and *Cooking Light* magazine, Green is known for her encyclopedic knowledge of every possible ingredient, its history, culture, and use in the kitchen and bakery and for her lively story-telling garnered during a lifetime of culinary travel. Green also leads culinary tours—her next is scheduled for October 2013 to Puglia, Italy, which she calls "the land of 1,000-year-old olive trees." Green's books have garnered high praise from critics, readers, and culinary professionals alike, including a James Beard award for *!Ceviche!: Seafood, Salads, and Cocktails with a Latino Twist* (Running Press, 2001), which she coauthored with Chef Guillermo Pernot. She is always happy to answer your culinary questions. For more information about Aliza's books and tours or to send her a message, visit her website at www.alizagreen.com.

# ABOUT THE PHOTOGRAPHER

**STEVE LEGATO'S** passion for photography has granted him the humbling opportunity to work with some of the most dedicated, passionate, and creative chefs you've heard of, as well as dozens you haven't heard of—yet. His photography has been featured in *Art Culinaire*, the *New York Times*, *Bon Appetit*, *GQ*, *Wine Spectator*, *Food Arts*, *Travel & Leisure*, and *Wine and Spirits*. He has photographed more than forty cookbooks, including *!Ceviche!* by Guillermo Pernot, which won a James Beard Award, and *Nicholas: The Restaurant*, which was nominated for the 2010 IACP Cookbook award for photography. He has been overheard, thinking aloud, "of sustenance and soul, a good soup is made." www.stevelegato.com

# INDEX

## A

Acquacotta Maremmana, 5, 83–84
Alaska Wild Salmon Chowder with Bacon, Leeks, and Dill, 12, 126–127

## B

bacon
  Alaska Wild Salmon Chowder with Bacon, Leeks, and Dill, 12, 126–127
  Caribbean Callalou Soup, 50–51
  freezing, 51
  Italian Chestnut Soup with Fennel and Marsala, 64–65
  New England–Style Clam Chowder, 12, 128–129
  Pennsylvania Dutch Bacon, Corn, and Potato Chowder, 130–131
Barthe, Louis, 44
Bean/Chickpea Stock, 8
Bean Soups
  Ceci e Tria (Pugliese Chickpea and Semolina Noodle Soup), 89–91
  Charleston Black Bean Purée with Madeira and Lemon, 93–95
  cooking tips, 88
  Greek Lentil Soup (Faki), 4, 96–97
  Pasta e Fagioli, 101–102
  Turkish Red Lentil Soup (Mercimek Çorbasi), 4, 98–99
beef
  Beef Kreplach, 23–27
  Rumanian Beet-Vegetable Borscht with Beef Brisket, 119–121
  Vietnamese Beef Broth, 111–112
  Vietnamese Pho Soup with Beef Brisket, 109–112
Beef Stock
  French Onion Soup, 76–77
  recipe, 7, 8
  Roman Stracciatella (Egg and Cheese Drop Soup), 40–41
  Zuppa Pavese, 4, 74–75
Benriner cutters, 5
Billi Bi, 44–46
bisques. See Potages, Purées, and Creamy Bisques.
Bouquet Garni, 49
broths. See Clear Broth-Based Soups; Fish and Seafood Soup/Stews; Roasted Chicken Broth; techniques; Vietnamese Beef Broth.

## C

Cacciucco Livornese, 47–49
Caribbean Callalou Soup, 50–51
Ceci e Tria (Pugliese Chickpea and Semolina Noodle Soup), 89–91
Charleston Black Bean Purée with Madeira and Lemon, 93–95
cheese
  Acquacotta Maremmana, 5, 83–84
  French Onion Soup, 76–77
  French Soupe de Potiron (Red Pumpkin Soup), 78–80
  Mexican Sopa de Tortilla with Shredded Chicken, 115–117
  Pasta e Fagioli, 101–102
  Roman Stracciatella (Egg and Cheese Drop Soup), 40–41
  Zuppa Pavese, 4, 74–75
chef's knives, 5
chicken
  Grandma's Jewish Chicken Soup with Kreplach, 22–27
  Mexican Sopa de Tortilla with Shredded Chicken, 115–117
  Pennsylvania Dutch Chicken Corn Soup with Rivels, 33–35
  Tom Kha Gai (Thai Chicken Coconut Soup), 31–32

chicken broth. See Roasted Chicken Broth.
Chicken Stock
  Caribbean Callalou Soup, 50–51
  Charleston Black Bean Purée with Madeira and Lemon, 93–95
  French Soupe de Potiron (Red Pumpkin Soup), 78–80
  Lobster Bisque with Cognac, 69–71
  Mexican Sopa de Tortilla with Shredded Chicken, 115
  Pappa al Pomodoro, 81–83
  Pasta e Fagioli, 101
  Pennsylvania-Dutch Bacon, Corn, and Potato Chowder, 130–131
  Pennsylvania Dutch Chicken Corn Soup with Rivels, 33–35
  Portuguese Caldo Verde, 113–114
  recipe, 9
  Sichuan Hot and Sour Soup with Duck, Watercress, and Tofu, 30
Chickpea Stock. See Bean/Chickpea Stock.
Chilled Soups
  Chilled Apricot Soup with Star Anise, 4, 134–135
  Chilled Melon, Yogurt, and Ginger Soup, 136–137
  Golden Tomato Gazpacho with Smoked Paprika, 4, 138–139
  Green Gazpacho with Garlic, Grapes, and Almonds, 140–141
China caps, 5
chinois, 5
Chowders
  Alaska Wild Salmon Chowder with Bacon, Leeks, and Dill, 12, 126–127
  New England–Style Clam Chowder, 12, 128–129
  Pennsylvania Dutch Bacon, Corn, and Potato Chowder, 130–131
  Scallop and White Corn Chowder with Roasted Poblano Chiles, 12, 124–125
Clear Broth-Based Soups
  broth straining technique, 145
  Grandma's Jewish Chicken Soup with Kreplach, 22–27
  Pennsylvania Dutch Chicken Corn Soup with Rivels, 33–35
  Roasted Chicken Broth, 20–21
  Roman Stracciatella (Egg and Cheese Drop Soup), 40–41
  Sichuan Hot and Sour Soup with Duck, Watercress, and Tofu, 28–30
  South Indian Tomato-Tamarind Rasam, 5, 36–39
  Tom Kha Gai (Thai Chicken Coconut Soup), 31–32
  Vietnamese Beef Broth, 111–112
cooking water, 7
Corncob Stock
  Corn Cream Soup with Summer Vegetables, 58–59
  Pennsylvania Dutch Chicken Corn Soup with Rivels, 33–35
  recipe, 10
Corn Cream Soup with Summer Vegetables, 58–59
court bouillon, 17
cremini mushrooms, 68
Creole Gumbo Z'Herbes, 106–108
Crostini, 49
Crunchy Fried Tortilla Strips, 118

## D

dough
Beef Kreplach, 23–27
Rivels, 35
Tria Pasta, 91
duck. See Sichuan Hot and Sour Soup with Duck, Watercress, and Tofu.

*E*

Egg and Cheese Drop Soup. *See* Roman Stracciatella.

*F*

Faki. *See* Greek Lentil Soup.
Fish and Seafood Soup/Stews
   Alaska Wild Salmon Chowder with Bacon, Leeks, and Dill, 12, 126–127
   Billi Bi, 44–46
   Cacciucco Livornese, 47–49
   Caribbean Callalou Soup, 50–51
   fish sauce, 32
   Lobster Bisque with Cognac, 69–71
   lobster roe, 151
   New England–Style Clam Chowder, 12, 128–129
   Provençal Soupe de Poisson with Rouille, 52–54, 55
   Rasam Powder, 38
   Scallop and White Corn Chowder with Roasted Poblano Chiles, 124–125
   Seafood Broth, 43
   Shrimp Stock, 11
fish pliers, 5
Fish Stock
   Alaska Wild Salmon Chowder with Bacon, Leeks, and Dill, 12, 126–127
   Billi Bi, 44–46
   recipe, 12
   Scallop and White Corn Chowder with Roasted Poblano Chiles, 12, 124–125
food processors, 5
freezer bags, 5
freezer gel packs, 5
French Onion Soup, 4, 76–77
French Soupe de Potiron (Red Pumpkin Soup), 78–80
fruit
   Bouquet Garni, 49
   Chilled Apricot Soup with Star Anise, 4, 134–135
   Chilled Melon, Yogurt, and Ginger Soup, 136–137
   Green Gazpacho with Garlic, Grapes, and Almonds, 140–141

*G*

Golden Tomato Gazpacho with Smoked Paprika, 4, 138–139
Grandma's Jewish Chicken Soup with Kreplach, 22–27
Greek Lentil Soup (Faki), 4, 96–97
Green Gazpacho with Garlic, Grapes, and Almonds, 140–141

*H*

ham. *See* pork.
Hearty Soups
   Creole Gumbo Z'Herbes, 106–108
   Mexican Sopa de Tortilla with Shredded Chicken, 115–117
   Portuguese Caldo Verde, 113–114
   Rumanian Beet-Vegetable Borscht with Beef Brisket, 119–121
   Vietnamese Pho Soup with Beef Brisket, 109–112
Hungarian Woodlands Mushroom Soup: Gombaleves, 66–67

*I*

ice cube trays, 5
Italian Chestnut Soup with Fennel and Marsala, 64–65

*J*

juicers, 5

*K*

kitchen string, 5
knives, 5

*L*

Leeks, William B., Jr., 44
Lobster Bisque with Cognac, 69–71

*M*

mandolines, 5
masking tape, 5
measuring cups, 5
Mercimek Çorbasi. *See* Turkish Red Lentil Soup.
Mexican Sopa de Tortilla with Shredded Chicken, 115–117
microplane zesters, 5
mushrooms
   cremini mushrooms, slicing and dicing, 68
   Hungarian Woodlands Mushroom Soup: Gombaleves, 66–67
   Mushroom Stock, 13
   porcini mushrooms, dried, 68
   Sichuan Hot and Sour Soup with Duck, Watercress, and Tofu, 30
   Tom Kha Gai (Thai Chicken Coconut Soup), 31–32

*N*

New England–Style Clam Chowder, 12, 128–129
nixtamalization, 118

*P*

packaged soups, 4
Panades
   Acquacotta Maremmana, 5, 83–84
   French Onion Soup, 4, 76–77
   French Soupe de Potiron (Red Pumpkin Soup), 78–80
   Pappa al Pomodoro, 81–83
   Zuppa Pavese, 4, 74–75
pancetta
   freezing, 51
   Italian Chestnut Soup with Fennel and Marsala, 64–65
Pasta e Fagioli, 101–102
Pappa al Pomodoro, 81–83
paring knives, 5
Pasta e Fagioli, 101–102
peelers, 5
Pennsylvania Dutch Bacon, Corn, and Potato Chowder, 130–131
Pennsylvania Dutch Chicken Corn Soup with Rivels, 33–35
pliers, 5
porcini mushrooms, 68
pork
   Alaska Wild Salmon Chowder with Bacon, Leeks, and Dill, 12, 126–127
   Caribbean Callalou Soup, 50–51
   Charleston Black Bean Purée with Madeira and Lemon, 93–95
   Italian Chestnut Soup with Fennel and Marsala, 64–65
   New England–Style Clam Chowder, 12, 128–129
   Pasta e Fagioli, 101–102
   Pennsylvania Dutch Bacon, Corn, and Potato Chowder, 130–131

Portuguese Caldo Verde, 113–114
  Smoked Pork Stock, 11
Portuguese Caldo Verde, 113–114
Potages, Purées, and Creamy Bisques
  Corn Cream Soup with Summer Vegetables, 58–59
  Hungarian Woodlands Mushroom Soup: Gombaleves, 66–67
  Italian Chestnut Soup with Fennel and Marsala, 64–65
  Lobster Bisque with Cognac, 69–71
  Senegalese Peanut and Yam Soup with Ginger, 60–61
  Tomato Bisque with Basil and Fennel, 62–63
pots, 4, 5
poultry
  Caribbean Callalou Soup, 50–51
  Charleston Black Bean Purée with Madeira and Lemon, 93–95
  Chicken Stock, 9
  French Soupe de Potiron (Red Pumpkin Soup), 78–80
  Grandma's Jewish Chicken Soup with Kreplach, 22–27
  Lobster Bisque with Cognac, 69–71
  Mexican Sopa de Tortilla with Shredded Chicken, 115–117
  Pappa al Pomodoro, 81–83
  Pasta e Fagioli, 101
  Pennsylvania Dutch Bacon, Corn, and Potato Chowder, 130–131
  Portuguese Caldo Verde, 113–114
  Roasted Chicken Broth, 20–21
  Roasted Chicken Stock, 7, 9
  Roasted Turkey Stock, 7, 9
  Sichuan Hot and Sour Soup with Duck, Watercress, and Tofu, 28–30
  Smoked Turkey Stock, 11
  Tom Kha Gai (Thai Chicken Coconut Soup), 31–32
  Turkey Stock, 9
Provençal Soupe de Poisson with Rouille, 52–54, 55
Pugliese Chickpea and Semolina Noodle Soup. See Ceci e Tria.
purées. See Potages, Purées, and Creamy Bisques.

R
Rasam Powder, 38
Red Pumpkin Soup. See French Soupe de Potiron.
Rivels, 35
Roasted Chicken Broth
  French Soupe de Potiron (Red Pumpkin Soup), 78–80
  recipe, 20–21
  Roman Stracciatella (Egg and Cheese Drop Soup), 40–41
  Sichuan Hot and Sour Soup with Duck, Watercress, and Tofu, 30
  Zuppa Pavese, 4, 74–75
Roasted Chicken Stock, 7, 9
Roasted Turkey Stock, 7, 9
Roman Stracciatella (Egg and Cheese Drop Soup), 40–41
Rouille, 54
Rumanian Beet-Vegetable Borscht with Beef Brisket, 119–121

S
Scallop and White Corn Chowder with Roasted Poblano
  Chiles, 12, 124–125
seafood. See Fish and Seafood Soup/Stews.
Senegalese Peanut and Yam Soup with Ginger, 60–61
Shrimp Stock
  Lobster Bisque with Cognac, 69–71
  New England–Style Clam Chowder, 128
  recipe, 11
Scallop and White Corn Chowder with Roasted Poblano
  Chiles, 124–125

Sichuan Hot and Sour Soup with Duck, Watercress, and Tofu, 28–30
sieves, 5
Smoked Pork Stock, 11
Smoked Turkey Stock
  Mexican Sopa de Tortilla with Shredded Chicken, 115
  recipe, 11
Soupmaker's Tips
  bacon, freezing, 51
  beans, cooking, 88, 92
  beef broth, storing, 112
  beef scraps, 8
  beets, handling, 121
  bread slices, flavoring, 77
  brisket, 112
  chilling soup, 144
  chorizo, 114
  cinnamon, 38
  coconut, grated, 37
  corn for Pennsylvania Dutch Chowder, 131
  curry leaves, 37
  fish for stocks, 12
  fish "frames," 55
  fish from Tyrrhenian Sea, 49
  fresh herbs, 146, 147
  gallinella (Tub Gurnard), 49
  greens, variety of, 108
  ham hocks, 95
  hoisin sauce, 112
  kreplach dough, 24
  mussels, 46
  pasta for Pasta e Fagioli, 102
  pumpkin, baking, 80
  red lentils, 99
  roasted chicken stock, 9
  roasted turkey stock, 9
  roux, color of, 108
  scallop "catch" muscles, 124
  scorfano nero (black scorpionfish), 49
  seafood broth, 43
  Sichuan peppercorns, 29
  Sriracha, 112
  sour cream, shaping, 135
  spider tool, 117
  squash, dicing, 58
  sumac spice, 99
  Thai ingredients, 32
  Tyrrhenian Sea fish, 49
  Urfa pepper, 99
  vegetable stock, 16
  water, adding to stock or soup, 121
  yams and sweet potatoes, 61
  zucchini, dicing, 58
soup pots, 4, 5
South Indian Tomato-Tamarind Rasam, 5, 36–39
spider tool, 5, 117
stocks. See Bean/Chickpea Stock; Beef Stock; Chicken Stock;
  Corncob Stock; Fish Stock; mushrooms; Roasted Chicken
  Stock; Roasted Turkey Stock; Shrimp Stock; Smoked Pork
  Stock; Smoked Turkey Stock; Soupmaker's Tips; turkey;
  Vegetable Stock.
storage containers, 5
sumac, 99

## T

Tamarind Purée, 39
techniques
  avocados, slicing, 152
  basil, cutting, 150
  *bouquet garni*, 149
  broth, straining, 145
  celery root, preparing, 152
  *chiffonade* technique, 100
  chilling soup, 144
  chives, cutting, 97
  clams, preparing, 129
  corn kernels, cutting off cob, 145
  dried beans, cooking, 103
  herbs, chopping, 147
  herbs, picking, 148
  leeks, cutting and cleaning, 153
  lobster roe, cooking and mashing, 151
  oil temperatures, 92
  onions, cutting, 151
  onions, studding with cloves, 148
  saffron threads, soaking, 149
  snow peas, julienne slicing, 146
  snow peas, preparing, 143
  thyme, tying into bundle, 153
  tomatoes, dicing, 150
Thai Chicken Coconut Soup. *See* Tom Kha Gai.
tips. *See* Soupmaker's Tips; techniques.
Toasted Garlic Croutons, 139
Tomato Bisque with Basil and Fennel, 62–63
Tom Kha Gai (Thai Chicken Coconut Soup), 31–32
tools, 5
Tria Pasta, 91
turkey
  Caribbean Callalou Soup, 50–51
  Grandma's Jewish Chicken Soup with Kreplach, 22–27
  Smoked Turkey Stock, 11
  Turkey Stock, 9
Turkish Red Lentil Soup (Mercimek Çorbasi), 4, 98–99

## U

urfa pepper, 99

## V

vegetable cooking water, 7
Vegetable Stock
  Alaska Wild Salmon Chowder with Bacon, Leeks, and Dill, 12, 126–127
  Billi Bi, 44–46
  Caribbean Callalou Soup, 50–51
  Charleston Black Bean Purée with Madeira and Lemon, 93–95
  Chilled Green Pea and Snow Pea Soup with Mint, 142–143
  Corn Cream Soup with Summer Vegetables, 58–59
  Creole Gumbo Z'Herbes, 106–108
  Golden Tomato Gazpacho with Smoked Paprika, 4, 138–139
  Greek Lentil Soup (Faki), 4, 96–97
  Pappa al Pomodoro, 81–83
  Pasta e Fagioli, 101
  Pennsylvania Dutch Bacon, Corn, and Potato Chowder, 130–131
  recipe, 14–16
  Scallop and White Corn Chowder with Roasted Poblano Chiles, 124–125
  Senegalese Peanut and Yam Soup with Ginger, 60–61
  Tomato Bisque with Basil and Fennel, 62–63
  Turkish Red Lentil Soup (Mercimek Çorbasi), 4, 98–99
Vietnamese Beef Broth, 111–112
Vietnamese Pho Soup with Beef Brisket, 109–112

## W

wire spiders, 5, 117

## Z

Zuppa Pavese, 4, 74–75